D1279025

Adult Guide
To
The Gift of Sexuality:
Empowerment for Religious Teens

Steve Clapp

A LifeQuest Publication

Adult Guide to
The Gift of Sexuality
Empowerment for Religious Teens

Steve Clapp

For further information, contact: LifeQuest, 6404 S. Calhoun Street, Fort Wayne, Indiana 46807; DadofTia@aol.com; (260) 744–5010.

The author of this book is not a medical professional. While every attempt has been made to ensure the accuracy of information about topics such as contraception, HIV/AIDS, and other sexually transmitted diseases, you should always depend on a physician for counsel on medical matters.

In portions of Chapter Six, the author has been heavily influenced by Debra Haffner's excellent sermon "Love Is the Spirit of This Church."

The names and/or locations of some persons quoted in this book have been changed to protect their privacy.

Biblical quotations are from the New Revised Standard Version of the Bible, copyrighted 1989 by the Division of Christian Education, National Council of Churches and are used by permission.

ISBN 1–893270–33–5

Library of Congress Control Number 2005936467

Manufactured in the United States of America

Contents

Part One:
Adults Only

Part Two:
Discussion Guide to *The Gift of Sexuality*

**This book is dedicated
to teenagers across the United States
who want to relate their faith
to their sexual decisions
and
to the clergy, youth workers,
and parents
who are seeking to help them.**

I feel a significant debt to many people who influenced the **Faith Matters** *project on which this book is based. I received especially significant guidance along the way from Jeremy Ashworth, Doug Bauder, Debra W. Haffner, and Martin Siegel. I have also been influenced by the work of others in related fields including Douglas Kirby, Diane di Mauro, and James Nelson.*

This book has been significantly influenced by the persons mentioned above and also by Marcia Egbert, Jan Fairchild, Dr. Dean Frank, Ann Hanson, Kristen Leverton Helbert, Jerry Peterson, Stacey Sellers, Holly Sprunger, Sara Sprunger, and Angela Zizak. The teens and adults who helped in the field testing process have significantly improved the quality of this book. My earlier collaboration with Julie Seibert Berman and Sue Brownfield continues to influence my work with teens.

The George Gund Foundation provided the primary funding for the development of this resource. Christian Community's work in the area of youth and sexuality has been helped by these foundations: The Compton Foundation, The Lutheran Foundation, and The Charles Stewart Mott Foundation. Related work has been helped by the Ford Foundation, the William and Flora Hewlett Foundation, the W.T. Grant Foundation, and the Robert Sterling Clark Foundation.

So now, O Israel, what does the LORD your God require of you? Only to fear the LORD your God, to walk in all his ways, to love him, to serve the LORD your God with all your heart and with all your soul, and to keep the commandments of the LORD your God and his decrees that I am commanding you today, for your own well-being.
Deuteronomy 10:12–13

Just then a lawyer stood up to test Jesus. "Teacher," he said, "what must I do to inherit eternal life?" He said to him, "What is written in the law? What do you read there?" He answered, "You shall love the Lord your God with all your heart, and with all your soul, and with all your strength, and with all your mind; and your neighbor as yourself."
Luke 10:25–27

Part One:
Adults Only

Chapter One:
Preparing Teens for
Sexual Decision-Making

I had a fascinating conversation with a Lutheran pastor and his fifteen-year-old daughter shortly after the publication of the book *Faith Matters: Teenagers, Sexuality, and Religion*. In that book, two colleagues and I shared the results of our study of 5,819 teens who are very involved in their congregations. The Lutheran pastor was a friend, and he was one of the first to read that book.

He and his daughter were visiting with me about the book as we stood in a shopping center in my hometown of Fort Wayne, Indiana. He said, "Now if I understand the statistics right, your research shows that about a fourth of the religious teens who are juniors and seniors in high school have had oral sex." His memory was good; the actual figures were 26.4% for females and 28.9% for males. He continued, "The youth group in my church has about 20 kids in it, and almost all of them are juniors or seniors. So that would mean that at least five kids in my youth group have had oral sex or will have it before they finish high school. Is that right?"

I explained that those were national statistics, and that there certainly were differences from congregation to congregation. Some had lower rates than that, and some had higher rates. "Well," he said, "I'm glad to hear you say that, because I just can't believe there are five kids in my youth group who've had oral sex."

His daughter gave him one of those looks that teens have when their parents are deemed completely out of touch with reality. "Dad," she sighed in exasperation, "a lot of the kids in the youth group and at school have had oral sex. I'd say it's way above 25% for our group. That's what you do to stay safe, to be faithful to the Bible. After all, when you have oral sex, you aren't really having sex, and you aren't going to get pregnant or get AIDS."

Her father had a shocked look on his face. I responded to his daughter, "Ummm, you have some misinformation there. You're right that you can't get pregnant from oral sex. But you sure can get HIV and other sexually transmitted diseases from oral sex unless you're using protection."

The color drained out of her face, and she said, "Are you serious?" I assured her that I was. Then she said, "Why doesn't anybody tell us this stuff? You could get killed not knowing that!"

And she was absolutely right. Not knowing that you can get HIV and other sexually transmitted diseases from unprotected oral sex can be fatal. And somebody should certainly be supplying that critical information to teens. Those somebodies are people like her father, other clergy, other parents, the author of this book, and the people reading this book.

Whether you live in Fort Wayne, Indiana; Brooklyn, New York; Selma, Alabama; Los Angeles, California; or Toronto, Ontario, you know that our culture has become increasingly focused on matters of sexuality. It pervades advertising, music, films, news reports, the hallways of our schools, and the Internet. Everyone who works with teens has to face the reality that the larger culture often gives young people exploitive messages and sometimes very inaccurate information. Many teens are involved in sexual behavior much earlier than their parents or their clergy would like to see. It is imperative that they have the knowledge needed to make healthy decisions about sexual behavior and to make those decisions within a spiritual context.

The fact that you have begun reading this book says some important things about you. First, you must be a person who cares about young people. Your perspective may be as a parent, teacher, a minister, a priest, a rabbi, a youth group leader, a teacher, a social worker, or another concerned adult.

Second, you are willing to face the reality that some young people are taking part in intimate sexual activities including oral sex and sexual intercourse. You know the lives of teens are likely to be far better if they don't take part in such intimate activities too early; and you are concerned about the potential for HIV, other sexually transmitted diseases, and unwanted pregnancy. You recognize that teenagers are developing their sexual values, and you want to equip them to make healthy sexual decisions. The research I was part of doing in the *Faith Matters* project shows that most young people want help as they prepare to face those decisions.

Third, your faith in God is important to you, and you want to see young people develop sexual values that are consistent with their faith. You recognize that parents and congregations have important roles to play in helping young people have the information and values needed for healthy sexual decisions.

My preparation for writing this book included directing the survey of 5,819 teenagers around the United States in which they were asked to share frankly about their religious faith, their congregational activity, their sexual values, and their sexual behaviors. I have shared many of the results of that study in *The Gift of Sexuality: Empowerment for Religious Teens*, to which the book you are currently reading is a companion. The full results of that research are published in the book mentioned earlier called *Faith Matters*. I've also had conversations with hundreds of young people to ask their guidance on the information they would like to have in a book written just for them.

That research has strongly confirmed that teens both need and want to receive information and guidance about sexuality from their parents and from their congregations. Most teens do not want to disappoint their parents, and those who are religious do not want to disappoint God.

Forming a sexual identity is an important developmental task for the adolescent years. My colleague Reverend Debra Haffner describes it this way in her excellent book *Beyond the Big Talk*:

> "First, during adolescence, children mature biologically
> into adults, developing the capacity to bear children
> themselves. Second, it is during these years that they
> experience their first adultlike erotic feelings, and
> almost all teens will begin to experiment with some
> sexual behaviors, alone and/or with a partner. Third,
> they develop a stronger sense of who they are as a man

or a woman (this is known as gender identity) and a stronger sense of their own sexual orientation (whether they are homosexual, heterosexual, or bisexual)" [p. 3].

We have a responsibility as adults to help them in that task.

Some of us have assumed that the brain was rather fully developed by the end of childhood, but neuroscience has shown this is not the case. The adolescent years are a time of significant change with the brain becoming more complex—especially in the location for higher functions like learning and socialization. The National Campaign to Prevent Teen Pregnancy has published an excellent report by Daniel R. Weinberger, Brita Elvevag, and Jay N. Giedd titled *The Adolescent Brain: A Work in Progress*. That report shares the intriguing description of an MRI study which

> "found that when identifying emotions expressed on faces, teens more often activated their amygdala—the brain area that experiences fear, threat and danger— whereas adults more often activated their prefrontal cortex—the area of the brain linked more to reason and judgment—and performed better on the task. Behaviorally, the adults' responses were more intellectual, the teens' more from the gut" [p. 2].

Thus there is strong evidence from neuroscience of the reality that teens need help from adults with decision-making. Teens have had only limited life experience in dealing with relationships and sexuality, and they are more likely to make decisions on an emotional basis than on a logical basis.

Seven Assumptions

There are seven important assumptions that provide the grounding for *The Gift of Sexuality: Empowerment for Religious Teens* and for this *Adult Guide*. (From this point on, I'll refer to the youth book as *The Gift of Sexuality* and to this book as the *Adult Guide*.) You may not agree with all of these assumptions, but knowing them will be helpful to you in considering the pages that follow.

One, I am convinced that both adults and teenagers need access to information about what teenage sexual

practices actually are and how teens feel about the sexual experiences they have had. Those of us who are adults need that information to jar us out of the complacency with which we have attempted to ignore this area of teen life.

Teenagers need access to information on sexual behavior for two reasons. First, without such information, it is too easy to assume that other teens are more sexually active than they in fact are. The study of 5,819 teens that I mentioned earlier (the *Faith Matters* study) shows that the range of expected sexual behavior for teens is very broad. **While some are engaging in sexual intercourse and oral sex, the majority of religious teenagers are not doing so.**

No one should be pushed into premature sexual activity on the basis that "everyone does it." Adults seeing the survey data for the first time tend to react with shock at how many teens have participated in oral sex and sexual intercourse. Many teens, however, are surprised that the percentages are not higher than they are. Knowing what others are actually doing helps one put in perspective what immediate peers claim "everyone" does. Knowing the mixed feelings that many teens have about early sexual activity can help other teens think more carefully about such decisions.

Second, many teenagers, like adults, find it far easier to talk about sexual behavior and values in terms of the survey results than in terms of their own experiences. In the area of sexuality, I can talk about what *others* do and believe more safely than about what I personally do and believe. As I have had opportunity to share the data from the *Faith Matters* study with youth groups, I have repeatedly found them willing to discuss the survey and the issues raised by the survey.

Two, teenagers have a right to direct access to accurate sexual information. When young people do not receive the information that they need, early sexual activity, teen pregnancy, abortion, HIV/AIDS, other sexually transmitted diseases, rape, and sexual abuse can all be a result. Young people pay a price when those of us in the religious community fail to take seriously our responsibility to them.

I am personally convinced that the majority of teenagers make responsible decisions when they are provided with accurate information. Both secular studies and the *Faith*

11

Matters study confirm that teaching young people about contraception and about sexually transmitted diseases does not make them more likely to engage in early sexual activity. **In the Faith Matters study, eight percent of responding congregations provided information about contraception. Those congregations reported no instances of teen pregnancy.** Youth from those congregations were not any more likely or less likely than other youth in the study to have had sexual intercourse. The provision of the information does not make them more likely to be sexually active but does give them protection if they are.

The United States is in the midst of a heated political debate over "abstinence only" versus "comprehensive sexuality education." Proponents of abstinence-only strategies feel strongly that teenagers are not ready for sexual intercourse and other intimate sexual activities. They are reluctant to provide them with information about contraception. It feels hypocritical to be saying "Don't have sexual intercourse until you are married" and also to say "But if you do, this is how to protect yourself."

The comprehensive sexuality education programs of which I am aware also have a strong abstinence message but include fuller information about sexuality, including contraception and the prevention of HIV and other sexually transmitted diseases. These approaches recognize the reality that some young people are going to have intimate sexual activities whether we as adults want them to or not—and they want teens to be protected against disease and pregnancy if they have those activities.

Let me be clear. I think that high school students should abstain from sexual intercourse and oral sex. Most adults feel the same way. But I think, for two primary reasons, that "just telling them *no*" doesn't do enough to protect them.

First, they need to know how sexual response works and to have comfort and skill in communicating about sexuality if they are going to succeed in abstaining. The *Faith Matters* study made clear that large numbers of teens have early sexual experiences because they succumb to social pressure or simply aren't able to communicate what they are and are not willing to do with another person. We have to provide them with the knowledge and skills they need in order to abstain from intercourse.

Second, there are some teens living in our highly sexualized culture who are going to choose to have intimate sexual activity no matter what you and I say to them. Those teens need to be protected against pregnancy, HIV, and other sexually transmitted diseases. If we haven't made that information available to them, then we put them at great risk. And teens grow into adults, who will virtually all be involved in intimate sexual activity. The teen years are an excellent time to equip them with the knowledge that they need about sexuality and also to provide them with the skills they need to be good marriage partners and good parents.

I find it significant that many countries do a better job of protecting their youth from pregnancy and disease than the United States does. This information comes from the Advocates for Youth organization, which does an excellent job staying current on what is happening with sexuality education in the United States and in other countries. In the Netherlands, the teen birth rate is over eight times lower than in the United States. In Germany, the teen abortion rate is nearly eight times lower than in the United States. In France, the teen gonorrhea rate is 74 times lower than in the United States (Yes, it really is 74 times lower . . . that is not a misprint!). Those countries are all less afraid than the United States of providing information on sexuality to their teenagers.

Parents and congregations need to do a better job of helping teens prepare for decision-making about sexuality, dating, marriage, and parenting. The *Faith Matters* study shows that most congregations are doing almost nothing; both those whose clergy want abstinence only and those whose clergy support a comprehensive approach.

For me personally, the case for comprehensive sexuality education is overwhelming; and my personal bias is that I think it needs to happen in the home and in congregational settings where it can be done in a spiritual context. When done in that way, I am convinced that it will result in less rather than more sexual activity on the part of teenagers; and it will also protect them against disease and unwanted pregnancy when they do become sexually active. As you read this *Adult Guide* and *The Gift of Sexuality* you will find strong messages urging teens to go slowly on sexual activity and to abstain from sexual intercourse and oral sex.

Three, teenagers who embrace the Christian or Jewish faith will make sexual decisions in a religious framework if supported by caring adults. Because decisions about dating, marriage, sexual activity, and parenting are moral and spiritual decisions, parents and religious institutions are the ones with the responsibility for imparting the beliefs, values, and information to shape those decisions. While there are important reasons for having sexuality education available through the public schools, it is not the job of public schools to impart the spiritual foundation that those of us in the religious community can offer young people in their decision-making.

In the *Faith Matters* study, we identified a subgroup of teens that was significantly less likely to have had sexual intercourse than the other teens in our study. Those teens (1,093 or 18.8%) share these characteristics:

- They attend religious services one or more times a week.
- They pray daily.
- They have involvement in at least one congregational group besides religious education and worship.
- They say that the teachings of the congregation and/or the Scriptures have "a lot of influence" on their sexual decisions.
- They say the congregation has provided information on how to make sexual decisions and on what the Scriptures says about sexuality.
- They feel a strong connection with congregational leaders who work with youth.
- They feel a strong connection with other youth in the congregation.
- They feel the adults who work with them portray sex in a healthy and positive way.
- They say their congregation encourages abstinence from intercourse for high school-aged people.

A strong connection to adults in the congregation; the provision of information on how to make sexual decisions; and the portrayal of sex in a healthy and positive way are strong contributing factors to these teens who were the least likely in the study to have had intercourse. The encouragement of abstinence was also a factor. Clearly caring adults in the congregation have a significant role to play.

Our study confirmed that teens want help from their congregations, and they want help from their parents in understanding how to make healthy sexual decisions. Parents have opportunity to have significant impact both by the quality of their own relationships with their teens and by their encouragement to the congregation to provide help to teens in this area of need.

Four, the Bible does not support the repressive view of sexuality that too many of us in congregations have attempted to impose on teenagers. Too many of us in the church and synagogue have been too quick to focus on a small number of biblical passages that are prohibitive in nature. We have not wanted to call attention to the kind of celebration of love and sexuality found throughout the Hebrew Bible and New Testament. We don't direct teens to the Song of Solomon. We have also not helped teens understand the implications of the scriptural teachings of love, grace, and forgiveness for intimate relationships with others.

When teens find the repressive view of sexuality that is so often presented by congregations in conflict with their own experiences and desires, increasing numbers reject the congregation's influence in this area of life. This may also cause them to reject the faith in other areas. Those of us who are adults need to help teens see that decisions about dating, sex, marriage, and parenting are, at the core, spiritual decisions.

Five, evidence exists from secular studies that short-term efforts at sexuality education are helpful but that many other factors are involved in helping lower early sexual activity by teens. How young people feel about themselves, how successful they are in school, and how connected they are with their family and significant adults can all have an impact on how early they commence sexual activity. In *No Easy Answers*, an excellent publication from the National Campaign to Prevent Teen Pregnancy, Douglas Kirby writes that for more impact, programs "need to effectively address a greater number of risk and protective factors over a long period of time" [p. 1].

Because churches and synagogues relate to children and their parents from the time of birth, there are numerous opportunities to help guide the development of young people in positive ways:

- Service projects and other experiences that help build the self-esteem of youth are a routine part of the life of many congregations.

- Worship and religious education help shape the spiritual lives and moral decision-making ability of youth.

- Relationships with clergy, teachers, youth workers, and other mentors in the congregation can have tremendous influence on the self-esteem and the values of youth.

If age-appropriate sexuality education is added to the many other positive experiences congregations make possible for youth, the potential exists for significant impact on their lives. Congregations are in fact ideal settings for sexuality education.

Six, the teachings of the Christian, Jewish, Muslim, Hindu, and Buddhist traditions include an emphasis on reaching out to people who are in need. The values of compassion, generosity, hospitality, and concern about justice are common to all the major faith traditions. Teen pregnancy, HIV/AIDS, and poverty are realities which people of faith would like to reduce. People who are pro-choice and people who are pro-life agree that there are far too many abortions in the United States.

Churches, synagogues, and other faith-based institutions can help not only their own young people but also young people in the community. With congregations in every neighborhood in the United States, there is tremendous potential for positive impact on these social problems if faith-based institutions can identify effective strategies. I hope *The Gift of Sexuality* can be a resource that will help congregations in that process. Because it can stand alone without the necessity of being used in a class or group, teens can be encouraged to give copies of it to their friends.

Seven, young people need information and guidance to help them prepare for relationships, dating, marriage, and parenting. While it is very important to provide young people with the factual information, the values, and the decision-making skills needed for healthy sexual choices, they need far more than that. Sexual decisions come within the context of relationships, and healthy sexual decision-making is difficult unless the relationships within which the decisions are made are also healthy.

The word *dating* does not mean the same thing to all young people, and some young people are not using the word at all. Commonly used substitutions include *going out* and *seeing.* Your community may have other variations. I will use the word *dating* at several points in this book because it is reasonably descriptive of the close relationships which most couples enter at some point in their lives. And dating generally precedes marriage and parenting.

Many young people in our society find themselves pregnant well before they are married, and they find themselves taking on the responsibility of parenting before they have even completed their education. We know as adults that young people who do not have children until after they are married and finished with their formal education are far more likely to have successful and meaningful lives.

The *Faith Matters* study found that most congregations do not do much better helping teens prepare for dating, marriage, and parenting than helping them prepare for sexual decision-making. While the institution of marriage is certainly going through transitions, it remains one of the fundamental social institutions of our society. Yet we do very little to prepare young people for marriage.

In the *Faith Matters* study, we found that clergy may offer marriage counseling after couples are engaged and that some congregations offer marriage preparation retreats for couples. Those efforts, however, come after people have made the decision about whom their marriage partner will be. Young people need and want help understanding the nature of marriage and understanding the difference between factors that cause initial attraction and factors that result in lasting relationships.

It's not uncommon for adults whose marriages end in divorce to say some variation on: "We should never have gotten married in the first place. We weren't right for each other." But our society does very little to help us think about the kind of person we should marry or about the kinds of attitudes and practices that make for a healthy marriage. Teens need to be taught these things *before* they have chosen a life partner.

17

Parenting may be the single most important job that many of us ever have. Yet our society as a whole does very little to prepare us to be good parents. Young people who fully understand the challenges of being a good parent are far less interested in taking on that role at an early age. Congregations have wonderful opportunities to help young people in this area. Thus *The Gift of Sexuality* and this *Adult Guide* seek to help young people not only with information, values, and skills for sexual decision-making but also with preparation for dating, marriage, and parenting.

Using *The Gift of Sexuality*

The Gift of Sexuality can be used in three primary ways:

1. *The Gift of Sexuality* can be given directly to teenagers for personal reading. The book has been written to be understandable and interesting to teens who read it without any further adult guidance. I have worked hard to be faithful to Scripture and to the major faith traditions. I hope that adults will be comfortable letting teens have direct access to the book.

2. Some parents may want to give this book to their teenagers as a basis for dialogue with them. This *Adult Guide* will help parents using that kind of approach.

3. The book can be used as the basis for small group, Sunday school class, fellowship group, or retreat study. The second part of this *Adult Guide* contains suggested activities and discussion guidelines for those who would like to use the book in that way.

For parents who want more background on talking to teens about sexuality than they find in this *Adult Guide*, I strongly recommend two excellent books by others. These are good resources for individual reading and also for study by groups of parents in a congregation or in the community.

Debra W. Haffner, *Beyond the Big Talk: Every Parent's Guide to Raising Sexually Healthy Teens from Middle School to High School and Beyond.* Newmarket Press, New York, 2001, 2002.

Sabrina Weill, *The Real Truth about Teens and Sex: From Hooking Up to Friends with Benefits—What Teens Are Thinking, Doing, and Talking About, and How to Help Them Make Smart Choices.* The Berkley Publishing Group; Perigree, New York, 2005.

Chapter Two:
Talking about Sexuality

Adults are often uncomfortable talking with youth about sexuality. In fact, that reality is why many good theories on sex education break down when it comes to application. In the *Faith Matters* study, we had many adults share comments like these:

> *Both of my kids are teens. I know that I should be talking with them about sex, but I feel so awkward with the topic. My husband and I don't even talk much about sex with each other; we just do it.*
> Roman Catholic Parent

> *I keep feeling like we should do a Sunday school unit on sex and the faith, but my anxiety has kept me from it. I know, in my heart and in my mind, that teens need guidance to avoid pregnancy and HIV. They also need guidance to claim sex as a good and natural part of their lives. But two things stop me. First, I'm afraid that I'll show my own ignorance by not knowing as much as I should. Second, I'm worried about flack from parents and adults in the church.*
> United Methodist Sunday School Teacher

> *Aside from commitment to Christ, there's probably no topic that's more important to talk about with teens than sex. But seminary doesn't offer any classes on how you go about doing that. How much should a person share? It isn't enough to just tell them NO. But is there a line somewhere on information sharing that you shouldn't cross?*
> Evangelical Lutheran Minister

> *I've started conversations with our daughter several times, and I've made it clear that my husband and I expect her to abstain from intercourse as long as she's living with us and that we think she should wait until*

*married to have sex. I know we should also talk with
her about contraception and HIV, but I don't know
how to go about it.*

American Baptist Parent

The Sociological Quarterly [#46, February, 2005] shares a study by Mark D. Regnerus titled "Talking about Sex: Religion and Patterns of Parent-Child Communication about Sex and Contraception." That study suggests that parents who are regular in attendance at worship are *more likely* than other parents to talk to their teens about the morality of sex but *less likely* to share factual information with them, especially about contraception. The study also notes that African-American parents discuss sex, contraception, and sexual morality with their teenagers more often than white, Hispanic, or Asian parents. Single parents are more likely than two-parent families to discuss sex, including contraception, with their teenage children.

You may be reading this book as a single parent, a part of a two-parent household, a clergyperson, a sexuality educator, a youth group advisor, a youth class teacher, or in some other role related to youth. Whatever your relationship with teens, some of these guidelines may be helpful to you in talking with youth about sexuality.

1. Practice talking with adults first. If you can't talk comfortably about sexuality with adults, you will probably have difficulty doing so with young people. Churches and synagogues can help by providing classes, workshops, or seminars on sexuality and the faith. Just talking with other adults about these concerns and about the need for sex education may help you feel more secure and comfortable talking with teens.

If you are a parent, seek opportunities to talk about teens and sexuality with your friends and with the parents of other teens. Tell them about this book. Share your concerns about the sexual values and behaviors of teens, and listen to the concerns that they have. You'll learn from them, and they'll learn from you. These don't have to be formal, organized conversations. Ask other parents if their teens have seen a particular movie or television show about which your teen is talking.

A group of adults preparing to lead youth classes on sexuality may find it helpful to have preliminary sessions of their own in which they go through *The Gift of Sexuality* and this *Adult Guide.* Talk with other adults about some of the suggested exercises. Confidence gained in that way will make it easier to discuss the same topics and to do the same exercises with youth.

Another helpful option can be that of running a class for parents and other adults simultaneously with a class for youth. Use the same basic materials. Adults who have offspring in the youth group will be aware of what their young people are discussing and will find it easier to visit with them.

Consider having a congregational study for parents and other adults based on the book *Faith Matters: Teenagers, Religion, and Sexuality.* That book gives a full report of the study on which this book and *The Gift of Sexuality* are based. A discussion guide is included in the back of *Faith Matters.*

Finally, just initiate conversations of your own about youth and sexuality with your spouse, with friends in the congregation, or with other adults who care about youth. Becoming comfortable discussing these topics with adults will help you have similar conversations with youth.

2. Decide in advance how much of your own experience you are willing to share. Youth can ask pointed questions of parents, clergy, and youth workers:
- "Did you have premarital intercourse?"
- "Did you sleep with anyone before Mom?"
- "Have you always been faithful to Dad?"
- "Did you really want to have four children, or did you have a problem with contraception?"
- "Did you ever think about having an abortion?"

You need to decide in advance just how open you are willing to be about your own experiences. Some young people will be more open with you if you risk sharing some of your personal experiences with them. At the same time, there are limits on how much any of us is willing to share. Do not make the mistake of assuming that the young people who share your home or with whom you work will think less of you because of something you share—they may think more of you because of your honesty.

A core question for parents to ask is:

*To what extent do your own
experiences and behaviors support
what you want your child to do?*

If you had sexual intercourse at the age of 13 and don't want your son or daughter to do the same thing, then it's probably a mistake to talk about having done so. On the other hand, if you got pregnant at the age of 15, your son or daughter can easily do the math and has probably already figured out what happened. In that case, you will want to talk about what you experienced and share the reasons why you hope your son or daughter does not do the same.

The one area that many young people seem unwilling to forgive is *extra*marital intercourse. Thus it is generally unwise to talk about extramarital sexual activity with teens. It also runs the risk of sounding hypocritical if a parent who has had extramarital intercourse (against the conventions of society) is urging a teen to avoid premarital intercourse (which is against the conventions of society). It is not necessary to "reveal all" in order to talk meaningfully about sexuality with youth. Do *not* however, expect your young people to share more of their own experiences with you than you are willing to share with them.

There are instances of divorced couples where extramarital intercourse played a factor in the divorce, and teenage children are often aware of that reality. If that is the case and your children bring it up, don't lie to them about it. Don't share more details that you feel comfortable doing, but be sure you are honest about what you say. It is also virtually never a good idea to say something that reflects negatively on the spouse with whom you are no longer living.

While many adults do not want to share the specifics of their own experiences and generally want to avoid any confession of premarital intercourse, some experiences may be easier to share. Here are statements of some parents and other adults that have been shared with teens:

*I could maintain control pretty well when I was just
kissing; but I always found it pretty hard to stop with
light petting. I'd want more.*

American Baptist Parent

*It's hard to think about birth control and disease
prevention when you're in the middle of touching and
kissing. My own experience has been that if I didn't
know in advance what I was going to do, I'd end up
taking chances. You have to plan in advance to take
the pill or use the patch, and you can't use a condom if
you don't have one with you.* Jewish Parent

*I often felt guilty over things that I'd think. I'd think
about having sex with a television star, with a hot guy
at school, with a teacher, and even with a member of
my family. I wish I'd understood earlier that having
fantasies is a normal thing.*

Assembly of God Parent

*I sometimes enjoy looking at Playboy and Playgirl.
The problem I see with those magazines and the
Internet is that the information in them isn't always
right. They also give you the impression that every-
body's having sex all the time, which just isn't true.*

Unitarian Universalist Parent

*I used to be afraid that my parents would catch me
masturbating. I felt guilty about it until I got to college
and discovered that almost everyone does it. It's
normal—nothing to feel guilty about or ashamed of.*

Disciples of Christ Parent

*A lot of things in our culture make it easy to feel like a
member of the opposite sex is just an object to be
manipulated and enjoyed. I sometimes think the
same way, but I know it isn't right. My faith in Christ
has helped me a lot there. If a person really tries to
see the presence of Christ in another person, it
becomes pretty hard not to recognize that you can't
have a relationship that is just physical.*

African Methodist Episcopal Parent

*I used to pray for God to help me get dates with a
person I really liked. I always felt silly when I did it.*

24

After all, God couldn't be concerned about my dating life. But that's not quite true. God did care about my dating life like he cares about every other part of any person's life. He may not have answered all my prayers in the way that I wanted Him to respond, but He does care. I think praying about my feelings did help me grow closer to God.

Presbyterian Parent

The preceding statements are just examples. You may want to share significantly more or significantly less. You do need to decide in advance how much you are willing to share. It's also good to remember that young people are just as uncomfortable as adults in sharing specific sexual experiences. Don't put them under more pressure than you want them to put on you.

3. Talk about statistics; case studies; TV programs; movies; the Internet; and magazine articles. These can provide "safe ground" for you and the young people with whom you work or live. TV programs and magazine articles can provide natural opportunities for conversation without any particular preparation. Take advantage of these opportunities whenever possible.

For young people and adults alike, it is far easier to talk about statistics or situations involving other people than about personal experiences. Yet the amount of learning and sharing which can come from this kind of discussion is significant.

One of my goals in writing *The Gift of Sexuality* was to provide material that youth and adults can discuss with relatively low risk. Many of the statistics and teen comments that have been included in that book are there for the purpose of stimulating discussion. Ask questions: Do *you* agree with this statement? Do you think young people in this community would have responded in the same way to the survey?

Talk with teens about the Internet sites they enjoy, the music they hear, the movies they see, and the magazines they read. Go see some of the movies they like; listen to their music; watch their television shows. A website called **screenit.com** provides information about how sexually explicit a movie is. There are obviously going to be some films that you don't want to approve of younger teens viewing. But as teens move on into high school, the effectiveness of prohibitions on movies and

25

Internet sites begins to decline significantly. Sometimes a better approach may be to talk with them about what they are viewing.

Consider the possibility of going with your teenage son or daughter to a movie that he or she wants to see. If you go together, you have the opportunity to visit before and after the movie about what they are seeing.

I know a parent, for example, whose daughter, a junior in high school, really wanted to see the movie *Kinsey*, which talks about the life and work of the famed sexuality researcher. At first the parent was alarmed at the idea of his daughter seeing such a movie. Then he realized that she was only two years away from being in college and going to see whatever she wanted. And he decided it would be a good opportunity to talk about sexual values and behaviors. They went to the movie together, and then they talked for two hours over pizza about the movie. He gained the opportunity to share his observations about what he considered both healthy and unhealthy practices shown in the movie, and he was surprised to find how interested she was in his opinions and how strongly she agreed with him on most things.

4. Learn to speak factually rather than emotionally about topics like contraception. It's of critical importance to be sure that young people have adequate information about disease prevention and contraception. Do whatever reading or study you need in order to be well informed on those topics. Do not *assume* that your young people already have adequate information.

In doing the research for the *Faith Matters* study and in working with youth on developing *The Gift of Sexuality*, I've repeatedly encountered questions about disease prevention and contraception from young people who tried to appear relatively sophisticated in sexual knowledge and experience. Many teens have inaccurate or incomplete information. Don't trust that they are getting the facts from other sources. The reality that they act sophisticated is no guarantee that they possess accurate knowledge.

The Gift of Sexuality provides considerable factual information on disease prevention and contraception. That can provide a basis for talking about those topics with teens. You'll also find that the daily news on television, in newspapers, and over the Internet provides many opportunities to bring up the topics. Teen pregnancy, new information about contraception, and statistics on the spread of HIV and other sexually transmitted diseases are certainly newsworthy topics. As we were going to press with *The Gift of Sexuality*, there were preliminary reports of new information from studies on the patch and the ring.

We have a tendency to get emotional when we discuss these topics with teenagers, whether it's a conversation taking place in a church youth group or between a parent and teenage child in the family room. As adults, we know a long list of reasons why it's better for people to wait until they are older before having such intimate activities as sexual intercourse and oral sex. We know the consequences of unplanned pregnancy, the danger of HIV and other sexually transmitted diseases, and the emotional issues involved in sexual relationships. We also know the close connection between sexuality and spirituality—that decisions about sexuality should not be divorced from the spiritual life. But when we get emotional in conversation with teens, they tend to shut down and stop listening to us.

And the truth is that teens do need this factual information. In most instances, it will not make them either more or less likely to have the early sexual experiences. It will keep them safe if they do so, and it will have them better prepared for such relationships later in life.

Here's a related and important matter for parents to consider. Most parents I know would prefer that their high school sons and daughters not be having oral sex or sexual intercourse. But if the teens are going to do so, would you prefer to have them sneaking around to get contraception and HIV/STD protection, or would you rather have them asking for your assistance in that process? If you would prefer to have them asking for your assistance, then it is important to communicate to them in advance that you always want to help them and that you never want them to take a chance on pregnancy, HIV, or another sexually transmitted disease. Make it clear that you are willing to help them with contraception and other protection when they are at the point that they intend to have intimate sexual activity with another person.

5. Seek to be nonjudgmental in talking about sex. You have a right to share your personal values and norms in the area of sexuality. Young people will respect you for saying how you feel. They will not, however, respect you if you are harshly judgmental or critical where their attitudes differ from your own. No matter how strongly you disagree with the attitudes expressed by youth, remember that you *cannot* make them believe as you do and that they ultimately have a right to their own values. Statements like these are guaranteed to shut off dialogue:

- "A Christian couldn't say something like that."

- "You have no right to talk like that. We raised you better than that."

- "That kind of attitude is sickening."

- "I don't ever want to hear you talk like that again."

- "If you really loved us, you wouldn't talk like that."

You certainly can share why you disagree with a young person, but share your reasons in a spirit of openness and respect for the young person.

Young people will sometimes make radical statements for the purpose of upsetting their parents or other adults. Adults who "fly off the handle" and display visible irritation have done exactly what they were programmed to do.

6. Learn to ask the right questions. Young people respond well if they find that you are genuinely interested in their attitudes and opinions. Ask about their attitudes and opinions rather than asking about their sexual activities. Questions like these are appropriate:

- "These statistics on premarital intercourse look a little high for our community. Do you really think that many young people have already had intercourse?"

- "A lot of the reading I've done makes me a little afraid of the patch as a form of birth control. Do you think many teens around here are using the patch?"

- "Do you think R ratings actually keep young people away from films? Do you think a teenager would see anything shocking or disturbing in an R-rated film?"

7. Practice listening to teens. Many young people almost desperately need contact with adults who will genuinely value their opinions and who will listen to their concerns. Parents and congregational youth workers have a tremendous opportunity if they simply take time to *listen* to teenagers. You don't have to agree to be genuinely interested in their opinions and observations. If you listen to them and show by your comments that you appreciate what they have to say, they will be far more likely to seek help and advice from you. Discipline yourself in the art of letting a young person (or any other person for that matter!) express a *complete* opinion or idea without interrupting to share your own input. As adults, we often feel so acutely the need to share our opinions and admonitions that we fail to give young people a chance to express their own views.

Remember that it's impossible to *make* a young person believe or think as you do. Trying to force your will on a young person guarantees that you will lose your influence. Learn to value their opinions; learn to enjoy listening to them; and you'll find them far more willing to listen to you. They need, want, and value the opinions of caring adults but they are threatened by and will likely reject our demands.

8. Don't be put off by long silences! Silence from a teenager or any other person can mean a variety of things. It may mean that the person has nothing to say at the moment. It may mean that the person is thinking carefully before responding. It may mean that the silence is being used as a weapon.

Don't overreact to silence. If you think a response is needed, just wait patiently. Most people, including teens, can't stay silent for long. They'll generally respond in time. If they choose not to respond, then respect their right not to do so.

Remember that it can appear they are using silence as a weapon when in reality they just aren't sure what to say or are feeling embarrassed by the conversation. If they are using silence as a weapon, then a strong reaction on your part will simply show that the weapon worked!

If it appears best to let their silence be the end of the conversation, then say you appreciated the chance to talk. Reinforce the fact that you are willing to visit about such topics anytime.

9. Use "I" language in talking with youth. Share your experiences and values—but make it clear that they are *your* experiences and values. Use lots of statements beginning with "I."

- I feel. . .

- I think. . .

- When I think about how God wants me to live, I. . .

- When you say that, I. . .

- I value your opinion about. . .

Avoid comments like these, unless you are absolutely certain of what you are saying:

- Everyone knows that. . .

- God does not want us to. . .

- No doctor will do that. . .

- Other young people don't get to. . .

- The Bible absolutely says that. . .

This doesn't mean that you should withhold your beliefs about how God, the Scriptures, and your religious traditions should affect sexual decision-making. It does mean sharing these as *your* beliefs rather than expecting a teenager to agree with everything you say. The more honestly and openly you talk and the more respectful you are of teens' opinions, the greater the probability that they will respect what you say.

When you are not completely certain of your factual information, always qualify statements as "in my experience," "in my judgment," and so forth. Be open to the possibility that you can learn as well as teach when you talk about sexuality with youth.

10. Let them know you are always willing to help. Let them know that you are always open to talking with them about sexual concerns. This is especially important advice for parents but also important for clergy and others who work with teens.

Most teens love their parents and want to be loved and respected by their parents. Thus many teens hide things like these from their parents:

- The fact that he or she is having oral sex or sexual intercourse with another person.

- The fact that she is pregnant.

- The fact that he has gotten someone pregnant.

- The fact that he or she has a homosexual orientation. (In the *Faith Matters* study, 46% of the teens with such an orientation had never told their parents.)

- The fact that he or she could be at risk for HIV or another sexually transmitted disease—or may actually have such a disease.

I remember my own mother and father saying clearly to me, when I was a teenager, "We will always love you, and we will always do anything we can to help you. Nothing that you do will ever make us love you less, and we will help you deal with any situation you should face in life. If you have a problem related to sexual activity or to alcohol or drugs or to law enforcement or to school, it won't change our love for you. We will always do our best to help you, and we hope you will always be honest with us."

Parents should also let their teens know they'll always come get them with no questions asked if they find themselves in an awkward situation. You might want to give them a code. Tell them, for example, "If I ever get a phone call from you and you call me Claudette, I'll know you want me to come get you, no matter what else you say in the conversation." That gives them a way to get help if they are in a difficult situation without having to give details over the phone. (This strategy needs modification if your own name actually is Claudette!)

Chapter Three:
Health and Appearance

Teens are growing up in a society obsessed with sex and appearance. It's no surprise that many young people hold negative views of their own bodies. Part of the problem is that they listen too much to those of us who are adults! Many of us don't like our bodies, and we vocalize those feelings. We feel too fat or too thin; too tall or too short; too small in the chest or too small in the penis; too big in the feet or too big in the hips; always tired or always hungry; never exercising enough or never sleeping enough. And so the list continues. Young people learn from us to be extremely critical of their bodies.

There are other influences, of course. Movies, television, and magazines have created definitions of beauty that teenagers compare themselves to and nearly always come up short. Young people need help recognizing that most people do not look like media personalities or advertising models.

Young people also compare themselves to one another. This is particularly difficult during puberty, because people change at such vastly different rates. There's always someone around who is taller or thinner or who has bigger breasts or a bigger penis. The comparison game is a losing one, but youth play it all the time.

Be realistic when talking to youth about physical appearance. Those who are slow developers can be helped by accurate information about variations in appearance and in rate of development. All youth can be helped to better understand the varieties of physical shape and stature. But a junior high boy who is shorter than all the girls in his class or a sophomore girl whose breasts are showing no signs of growing beyond the kernel stage may not be easily convinced that all will work out fine over the next three to seven years. The frustration of the present is just too great. They can, however, be helped to feel at least somewhat better about themselves and to better understand what is happening in their physical development.

We should not take for granted that young people have the factual information they need about their bodies. In the *Faith Matters* study, for example, we found that many teens, both male and female, do not fully understand menstruation. When we field-tested *The Gift of Sexuality*, we had large numbers of males and females sharing appreciation for that kind of factual information.

As adults, we often feel horrified if we hear young people using words like tits, cock, cum, jerking off, giving head, screw, and clit. It is important not to overreact to the use of slang by young people. In fact, they often use slang words for the specific purpose of getting a reaction out of adults or out of other teens. Getting visibly or verbally upset about the language of a young person may be responding precisely as one has been programmed.

The words we use are important. Slang language poses two significant problems in communicating about sexuality. First, it is easy to become confused about what those terms actually mean. In some parts of the country, the word "cherry" refers to the hymen; in some other areas, it refers to the clitoris; in yet other areas it is a general term for virginity; and in one community (of which I am aware) it refers to the nipple on a woman's breast (but not on a man's breast).

The second problem is the more significant one. The words that we choose often reflect the respect that we feel for our bodies and the bodies of others. As you talk with young people about sexuality, try to help them use the more technical terms and model that behavior in your own choice of words.

Like the rest of society, teenagers are not necessarily as obsessed over improved health as they are over physical appearance. Most of them need guidance on nutrition, exercise, and healthy habits. You'll find considerable information in Chapter Four of *The Gift of Sexuality*.

In addition to providing information about healthy eating, homes and congregations should provide good examples. Youth groups should not continually serve snacks that are high in sugar, grease, or fat. Though young people will initially grumble if served more nutritious snacks, they can develop a taste for fresh fruits, cheese, and low sugar drinks.

Some Other Considerations

Here, as in other chapters in this *Adult Guide*, I want to avoid unnecessary duplication of information contained in *The Gift of Sexuality*. There are four other areas of particular concern to parents and other concerned adults that I do want to raise in this chapter:

1. Adults should be alert for signs of *anorexia nervosa* and other eating disorders. Anorexia is probably the best known of these disorders and is especially associated with teen females. Young people with that disease generally "see" themselves as much heavier than they are and almost literally starve themselves in a compulsive effort to lose weight. Young people suffering from that disease need professional help. You will *not* successfully treat that disease without the guidance of a skilled physician or mental health provider.

It's also important to be aware that teenage males can also have eating disorders. If you see signs of significant weight loss or weight gain in a teenager, it's important to find out what's happening. It's better to risk offending a teen by questioning what is happening than to ignore a situation later and be broken-hearted. Here's what one mother shared in a focus group as part of the *Faith Matters* study:

Our daughter was down to eighty-two pounds before we realized how serious the situation was. She had been wearing more loose fitting, long-sleeved clothes, and we had gradually gotten used to her being a lot thinner. But one day I accidentally walked in on her in the bathroom and saw that her arms and legs were like sticks. I mean, she looked like a prisoner of war. It was just awful. I took her straight to the doctor, and it took her three years to get well. If only we had paid attention to what was happening earlier.

2. Teenagers need to be involved in regular exercise. Competitive sports are not for everyone, and the medical community has some differences of opinion as to how "healthy" some competitive sports, especially football, really are. *All* young people, however, can benefit from a program of regular exercise—whether practiced as an individual, with a group at school, or with a church or synagogue group.

Some congregations have had considerable success in forming early morning youth jogging groups; mother/daughter swimming groups; father/son gymnastic groups; or family exercise clubs. If a parent and a teenage son or daughter are both feeling too fat or out of shape, joint participation in an exercise program may be of significant value both in improving health and in improving communication. Remember, however, that an out-of-shape adult cannot get into shape as quickly as an out-of-shape teenager.

3. You need to be concerned about use of tobacco, alcohol, and illegal drugs by teens. Chapter Four in *The Gift of Sexuality* builds a strong case for teens abstaining from these substances. As a parent, you want to share your values concerning these substances. You also need to be aware that what you do conveys at least as much as what you say. If you smoke yourself or drink alcohol excessively, you should not be surprised if your own children or the teens who are around you do the same.

Our society is guilty of fairly deep hypocrisy where illegal drugs are concerned. While there are many very important reasons not to use marijuana or cocaine, the reality is that the health risks from these substances is probably not greater than the health risks from tobacco and alcohol, which are legal in our society based on the age of the user.

You will not get far with most teenagers arguing that illegal substances are worse for their health than tobacco or alcohol. You can, however, argue quite convincingly that the very fact that these substances are illegal adds risks of other kinds to their use—the risk of associating with criminals who sell them and the risk of going to prison if caught with illegal drugs.

Some teens are going to experiment with alcohol no matter what you or I say. Be sure to convey to teens that it's especially important than they never drive after having even one drink. If they are going to drink with friends, there should be a designated driver who does not drink. Caution them never to get in a car with a person who has been drinking. If you are a parent, make it clear to your son or daughter that you are always willing to come get them, anytime, anywhere, rather than have them drive after drinking or ride with a driver who has been drinking.

As with sexuality, seek opportunities to convey your values in this area to teenagers. Tragically, almost every week brings news stories about deaths from drunk drivers, about persons arrested for drug deals, and about the impact of tobacco on health. Use those as opportunities to talk about these topics.

4. Young people also need help in recognizing that physical appearance is only one aspect of who we are. While there may be some limitations on how positively we can help them feel about their appearance, we have lots of room to help them feel good about themselves in other areas. Religious faith can make a major contribution to improving the self-image of teens and adults. Young people need to recognize God's love for them, and they experience (or fail to experience) that love in large measure through the way other people regard them. Help them cultivate their strengths, reinforce them for their accomplishments, and help them develop skill in reinforcing the worth of others.

While physical appearance obviously has much to do with the initial sexual attraction between people, physical appearance plays a much smaller role in the development of a meaningful and permanent relationship. More about this later!

Chapter Four:
Slowing Things Down

Sexuality is a very powerful part of our lives, and sexual relationships are complex. The responses to the *Faith Matters* study make it clear that many young people are having oral sex and sexual intercourse at earlier ages than those of us who are adults would like to see. Here are the statistics on the percentage of congregationally involved teens who have had intercourse and oral sex:

Intercourse and Oral Sex

	Intercourse	Oral Sex	Intercourse and/or Oral Sex
9th–10th Males	12.7%	11.4%	17.3%
9th–10th Females	14.7%	13.6%	19.5%
11th–12th Males	30.9%	28.9%	38.7%
11th–12th Females	29.0%	26.4%	37.6%

Those figures are considerably higher than most parents and clergy expected we would find among religious teens. The *Faith Matters* study also found that by the 11th and 12th grades, 70.9% of females and 71.6% of males have been involved in petting (fondling a partner's breasts and/or genitals). About half of both males and females in the 11th and 12th grades have been nude with a member of the opposite sex. Chapters Six and Seven of *The Gift of Sexuality* include additional statistics and quotes from teens about the extent of their sexual activity. You'll want to read those chapters carefully to get an idea of the diversity of experiences that teens have.

Thirty-one percent of 11th and 12th grade females and 12% of 11th and 12th grade males have had unwanted sexual experiences. Those unwanted experiences were more likely to result from social or emotional pressure than from physical pressure.

We also had reports from teens about events called "chicken parties" and "spin-the-bottle parties." While our research suggests that these activities occur more in some parts of the country than in others, the fact that they exist is disturbing. The chicken party name comes from a group of girls performing oral sex on a group of boys with the heads of the girls bobbing up and down like chickens. Spin the bottle parties, which once meant giving a kiss to the person on whom the bottle landed, can now mean giving oral sex to the person on whom the bottle landed.

Fifty-five percent of the teens in the *Faith Matters* study did not know that one can get HIV and other sexually transmitted diseases from oral sex. Chicken parties and spin-the-bottle for oral sex games are the exception, but the overall attitude of these teens toward oral sex is distressingly casual.

The reality is that many of these teens are not necessarily convinced that premarital intercourse and oral sex are "wrong." Here are the percentages of teens in the study who agreed with each of several statements about these activities:

92.8%   My faith community believes that premarital intercourse is wrong.

67.3%   The Scriptures of my faith teach that premarital intercourse is wrong.

54.1%   I personally believe that premarital intercourse is wrong.

65.4%   My faith community believes that oral sex before marriage is wrong.

34.7%   My faith community believes that oral sex is wrong even for people who are married.

18.9%   The Scriptures of my faith teach that oral sex before marriage is wrong.

28.7%   I personally believe that oral sex before marriage is wrong.

As adults, we know there are many problems with early sexual activity on the part of teenagers. It is, I am convinced, possible for parents and congregations to lower the probability of early sexual activity by teens. Doing so requires a willingness to talk with teens about these issues, to share the beliefs and values that adults hold, to give teens the information that they need, and to be willing to listen and respond to the questions teens have.

The *Faith Matters* study made it clear that, for sexually active teens, congregational involvement did not provide any immunity to pregnancy, HIV, or other sexually transmitted diseases. That's why it's important for teens to be provided the factual information that they need to be safe if they do take part in early sexual activity.

Pledges

Many congregations and community groups have utilized pledges as a way to encourage teenagers not to have sexual intercourse until after they are married. Although 19% of the youth responding to the *Faith Matters* survey have taken a pledge to remain a virgin until marriage, that group was not any more or less likely than others in the study to have had sexual intercourse or to have experienced or caused pregnancy.

That finding seems in conflict with a report by Peter Bearman and Hannah Brückner based on an analysis of teenagers in the National Longitudinal Study of Adolescent Health. Their report, published in the *American Journal of Sociology,* indicates that teens who made virginity pledges delayed sex about eighteen months longer than others. In my opinion, there are at least three reasons for the apparent difference.

First, our study looked at formal virginity or abstinence pledges as one of several religious variables. Most youth in our sample were highly religious, so the relative impact of the pledge might be expected to be different than in the more secular sample of the National Longitudinal Study.

Second, the overall frequency of sexual intercourse among the teenagers in our study was much lower than most other studies have reported. The impact of a pledge might well be different on these youth.

Third, the impact of the pledge, as reported by Bearman and Brückner, is greatest when it is not too popular in the school—when forty or fifty percent of a school takes the pledge, it no longer has impact. We can't speak to the school situation from our data; but most of the youth in our sample who took such a pledge were in a congregation in which most of the other teens did so—in fact there was tremendous peer pressure for them to take that step.

A recent study by Janet Rosenbaum of the Harvard School of Public Health found that teens who sign a pledge and then go on to have premarital intercourse are likely to later disavow having made such a pledge. This gives some indication of how difficult it is to get reliable information about the impact of these promises.

Other analysis of the National Longitudinal Study by Bearman and Brückner shows that teens who have made pledges are less likely to use condoms or other contraception when they do have their first intercourse. This raises additional concerns about the emphasis on pledges that has been made in some communities.

In doing research for this book, one of my Christian Community colleagues and I spent hours researching pledges and their results on the Internet. It's interesting to find that the data from Bearman and Brückner gets quoted both as proof that the pledges are effective (by delaying first intercourse) and as proof that the pledges are dangerous (because those who make them are less likely to use condoms or other contraception when they do have intercourse). The political agenda of those doing the reporting seems to affect the conclusions they draw and the emphasis they make.

Virginity pledge programs have become very popular among some constituencies in North America. To me, such pledges can serve a useful purpose and can garner strong community support; but it is dangerous to rely exclusively on these pledges to protect teens. The pledges may cause them to delay sexual intercourse, but substantial numbers of teens and young adults who have made pledges are still going to have intercourse before they are married. When they do have intercourse, they need protection against pregnancy and against HIV and other sexually transmitted diseases. I want to share a couple of important recommendations for those who work with virginity pledge programs:

- Consideration should be given to providing more comprehensive sexuality education along with the promotion of abstinence and virginity pledges. The young people who made the pledges and still had sex certainly would have benefited from more information about topics like contraception and sexually transmitted disease prevention.

- Congregations that encourage virginity pledges need to be aware of the fact that not all who make the pledges will end up keeping them. Discussions with teens need to cover acceptance, forgiveness, and second chances.

Given that the data from the *Faith Matters* study showed that religious teens who made pledges were not any more likely or less likely than other teens to have had sexual intercourse and to have experienced or caused a pregnancy, it seems to me a serious mistake to rely exclusively on such programs in work with religious teens. They need far more guidance, information, and help from their parents and from their congregations.

Pregnancy, Abortion, and Sexually Transmitted Disease

Among the teens in our study who are having sexual intercourse, 27.4% did not use any form of contraception the first time; and 19.5% did not use contraception the most recent time. Thus it is not surprising that some youth who participate in faith-based institutions have been pregnant or have gotten someone pregnant (percentages of all youth; not just sexually active youth):

	9th–10th Grades	11th–12th Grades
Male	1.6%	3.1%
Female	1.8%	2.8%

When the percentages are looked at in terms of the youth who are having intercourse, they become more alarming with 12.9% of sexually active 9th–10th grade females and 9.9% of sexually active 11th–12th grade females reporting a pregnancy. It is also important to note that some females active in faith-based institutions who become pregnant may drop out of activity in the faith-based institution and thus are not part of our data.

Half of the females responding to the survey who had become pregnant had an abortion. Several teens who had abortions commented that it was the only acceptable alternative given the views of their families and congregations about unwed mothers.

There were almost no pregnancies reported among those involved in Jewish or Islamic congregations, and those sub-groups also had the lowest rates of sexual intercourse. Jewish youth having sexual intercourse virtually all used contraception. Jewish congregations were not more or less likely than Christian congregations to have provided information on contraception. According to the survey responses of youth, Jewish parents were more likely than Christian parents to have provided that guidance to their teens. The Islamic youth were not likely to have received information on contraception from their congregations or their parents, but the numbers of those youth having intercourse were very low.

Youth from congregations that did supply information about contraception (about 8% of responding congregations) reported no instances of pregnancy. Youth from those congregations were not any more likely or less likely than other youth in the study to have had sexual intercourse. **The provision of information on contraception by the congregation does not make teens more likely to be sexually active but does give them protection if they are.** Studies on samples of secular teens have produced similar results—providing information to teens doesn't make them more sexually active but does give them important protection.

Being involved in a congregation gives no automatic protection against pregnancy, and it also gives no automatic protection against HIV and other sexually transmitted diseases. In the *Faith Matters* study, 9% of those who were sexually active reported having contracted a sexually transmitted disease.

We found teens in the *Faith Matters* study to be sadly deficient in the information they needed to have both to avoid pregnancy and to avoid HIV and other sexually transmitted diseases. The survey included the following true/false statements related to factual information about contraception.

The figures are the percentages of teens that answered each question correctly. The correct factual answer is provided in brackets.

% Answering Correctly	True or False Item

74%   The pill protects against HIV and other STDs. [False. It offers no protection against HIV and other STDs.]

66%   A woman can get a shot every three months that offers protection against pregnancy. [True. Depo Provera is a shot that is almost 100% effective at preventing pregnancy. The failure rate is less than 1%.]

73%   Condoms fail too often to be worth using. [False. Correctly used, condoms work 95 to 98% of the time.]

87%   If you put a condom on incorrectly or use the wrong kind of lubricant with it, the condom will not be effective. [True. Because of this, the actual user effectiveness of condoms is 86% to 90% rather than the higher effectiveness that is possible.]

26%   There is no emergency contraception or "morning after" pill or pills that can prevent pregnancy. [False. Emergency contraception within 72 hours of unprotected sex can prevent pregnancy 72 to 75% of the time.]

76%   The pill isn't very effective in preventing pregnancy. [False. The pill, taken daily, is 98 to 99% effective.]

68%   The pill often has side effects that are fairly serious. [False. The pill has been proven one of the safest drugs a person can take over the years. It may even protect against ovarian and uterine cancer. Some types of the pill help acne. Most women do not gain weight on the pill.]

When asked, "Do you know everything you need to avoid getting AIDS?", only 8.5% of the teens indicated that they did. Virtually all of the teens in the study lacked important information on avoiding HIV/AIDS and other sexually transmitted diseases.

Slowing Things Down with Healthy Communication

As shared earlier in this book, in the *Faith Matters* study, we did identify a subgroup of teens that was significantly less likely to have had sexual intercourse than the other teens in our study. Among 11th and 12th grade males in the study who had these characteristics, only 16.5% have had sexual intercourse, in contrast to 33.9% of the males who did not have all these characteristics. Among 11th and 12th grade females, the respective percentages were 15.8% and 31.6%. Those teens (1,093 or 18.8%) share these characteristics:

- They attend religious services one or more times a week.
- They pray daily.
- They have involvement in at least one congregational group besides religious education and worship.
- They say that the teachings of the congregation and/or the Scriptures have "a lot of influence" on their sexual decisions.
- They say the congregation has provided information on how to make sexual decisions and on what the Scriptures says about sexuality.
- They feel a strong connection with congregational leaders who work with youth.
- They feel a strong connection with other youth in the congregation.
- They feel the adults who work with them portray sex in a healthy and positive way.
- They say their congregation encourages abstinence from intercourse for high school aged people.

The encouragement of abstinence is a factor, but it is only one factor for this group of youth who were especially unlikely to have had intercourse. All of the factors are positive in nature: strong attendance and involvement, strong connections with other youth and with adults who work with youth, the provision of information on sexual decision-making, and what they see as a healthy and positive view of sexuality on the part of adults who work with them.

Those congregations were more willing to talk with teens about the process of sexual decision-making and were clear with teens about the teachings of their faith tradition. When one adds to that the earlier shared information that there were no instances of pregnancy in congregations that shared information about contraception, it becomes clear that a willingness to discuss these matters is key to keeping youth safe.

The reality is that the best way to slow down sexual activity on the part of teens and to keep them safe if they do take part in sexual activity is by providing information to them and talking with them about these concerns. Here are some guidelines that may be helpful both to parents and to leaders in congregations:

1. Teens need help from adults in understanding the complexity and the spiritual dimension of sexual relationships. From a religious perspective, sexual relationships need to develop gradually as people better understand each other, better communicate with each other, and better love each other. There *are* a lot of options besides kissing and having sexual intercourse. In fact, a whole lot should happen between the time that a couple kisses and the time that same couple experiences intercourse. The second guideline speaks more about this.

In *The Gift of Sexuality,* I've shared some of the sexual experiences that teens have had. The reality is that many teens felt awkward and did not enjoy intercourse or oral sex because they were not ready for that level of intimacy.

And sexual intercourse is not just a physical relationship. There is a spiritual dimension that is always present. When a man and a woman have intercourse, their relationship has been changed. It may have been changed for the better; it may have been changed for the worse. If the intercourse grows out of genuine love and respect for each other and reflects tenderness and kindness, then the change in the relationship is likely to be a positive one. If the intercourse grows out of physical attraction alone and involves the desire of one or both partners to "control" the other, then the relationship has been changed for the worse.

2. Help teens understand that sexual relationships need to be developed in a gradual way, over a period of time. Couples should not participate in sexual activity before having reached a comparable level in their ability to communicate with each other and to show concern for each other. Pages 57 through 60 in Chapter Five of *The Gift of Sexuality* provide a detailed discussion of a gradual approach to sexual intimacy. When we field-tested *The Gift of Sexuality*, we found that teens greatly appreciated this kind of clear guidance on going slowly.

Hugging, deeper kissing (often called French kissing), fondling, being nude together, manually stimulating each other to orgasm, and oral sex may all be a part of the activities that people experience before having intercourse. Those are also activities through which they learn more about their bodies and how to express caring to each other.

As shared several times in this book and in *The Gift of Sexuality*, oral sex certainly carries the danger of HIV and other STDs, and teens need to know about that danger and how to protect themselves. As adults, we should be willing to recognize that the choice to have oral sex by some teens is both a choice to avoid the danger of pregnancy and a choice to refrain from intercourse, which they believe their parents and congregations want them to do. If you personally believe that oral sex is wrong for teens, then it is important to convey your beliefs and the reasons for them to the teens with whom you live or work.

On page 58 of *The Gift of Sexuality*, I make a statement which some of my colleagues have challenged:

> **Remember that you can enjoy a long-term dating relationship and never move beyond light kissing. Our culture tries to convince us this is not true, but it is.**

The argument of my colleagues is that this is an unrealistic statement for teens today. The data from the *Faith Matters* study, however, does show that there are teens in long-term relationships who do not move beyond light kissing. There were also teens in focus groups who talked about needing the affirmation that there is nothing abnormal in not going beyond light kissing.

Whatever you and I as adults would prefer, however, the *Faith Matters* study does show that the majority of religious teens in the 11th and 12th grades are going to experience greater intimacy than light kissing. We need to recognize this reality and talk openly about it with teens. The better teens understand their own sexuality and the process of sexual arousal, the more likely they are to believe that a long-term dating relationship does not have to include sexual intercourse or oral sex.

3. Teens need to receive factual information about sexual arousal, contraception, HIV, and sexually transmitted diseases. *The Gift of Sexuality* speaks very frankly about these topics and provides teens with considerable information. I strongly recommend that you read Chapters Five, Six, Seven, and Eleven in that book so that you are current yourself on factual information on these topics. Having this information will not make teens more likely to have intercourse or oral sex, but it will keep them safe if they choose to do so.

4. Teens need to be reminded of the mathematics of sexual relationships. Many teens, feeling strongly attracted to another person and wanting sexual intimacy, fail to think about how a sexual relationship binds one to the entire sexual history of another person. For example:

- Bob and Annie just had intercourse with each other.
- Last year they each slept with four other people. [4 + 4 = 8]
- The year before that each of those people slept with three other people. [8 X 3 = 24]
- The year before that each of those people slept with three other people. [24 X 3 = 72]
- Thus Bob and Annie have slept with people who have slept with other people, making a total of 104 [8 + 24 + 72 = 104].
- That means that the risk of a sexually transmitted disease relates to all 104 of those people, not just to Bob and Annie.

This kind of example makes very clear why protection against HIV and other STDs is so critical. The use of protection stops or significantly reduces the risk of disease transmission.

47

5. Teens need to know that it's okay to say NO to any form of sexual expression. Reinforce to them that they are in charge of their own bodies and that no one else has a right to push them into any activity that they do not want to do. They also need to respect the bodies of others and be sure that they are not guilty of forcing or manipulating someone else into early activity. Chapter Ten of *The Gift of* Sexuality is devoted to the topic of unwanted sexual activity and helps teens recognize the great harm that is done when people are manipulated or forced into things for which they are not ready.

One of the major reasons for sharing so much statistical information and quotes from other teens in *The Gift of Sexuality* is to help young people see that "normal" sexual activity for teenagers covers a very broad range. People who tell them that "everyone" has oral sex or intercourse are not telling the truth.

Many people have intercourse and other forms of sexual activity for unfortunate reasons like these:

- As an attempt to cure their loneliness.
- Out of a desire to increase popularity.
- Because they do not want to hurt the feelings of another person.
- Because they are afraid of losing a relationship.
- Out of concern that they not appear homosexual.
- As a way of asserting independence from adult authority.
- In the hope of having a romantic relationship like those portrayed in movies and on television.

Those are not good reasons for sex with another person. In fact they are very bad reasons.

6. Teens need to be reminded that whenever they begin a new dating relationship, they should "return to square one." They should start over with a handshake or a good night kiss rather than attempting to pick up where they left off in their last dating relationship. They need time to know and understand the other person and to be understood by that person. They need time to develop comfort in communicating with each other. They need time to be certain how they both feel about their relationship and about sexual activity.

7. Help teens recognize that our culture puts lots of pressure for early sexual activity on teens and young adults. This pressure is especially hard for middle school/junior high youth. In general, middle school/junior high youth need a lot of group dating and group contact with the opposite sex.

High school students find that classmates, the Internet, movies, and television can all create pressure for sexual activity. They need to recognize that pressure and to think clearly about their faith, their values, their hopes, their dreams, and their respect for themselves and the other person.

These pressures don't end with graduation from high school. In some ways the expectation of sexual activity can be even stronger on college students, people in the military, and people who have begun full-time jobs. Being older does not necessarily mean that sexual activity should come faster. While young adults have generally had more sexual experience than high school students, that doesn't change the need for clear communication with the other person and living consistently with one's faith and values.

8. Remember that all of us have trouble with negative self-images. No matter how secure we are or how much we have accomplished, all of us have times when we have low opinions of ourselves. We may dislike certain aspects of our appearance or how we do in school or a career or how we communicate with others. We may dislike how other people tend to respond to us. We may dislike obsessive patterns of thinking that we have or our inability to be more disciplined.

Both teenagers and adults need to be careful that negative self-images do not lead us to behaviors we'll later regret. A male with a poor self-image may well seek to prove himself or feel better about himself by the sexual conquest of another person, whether he actually wants a particular sexual experience or not. A female with a poor self-image may well be afraid to say NO for fear of rejection. This is not to say that it is always the male who seeks sex and the female who decides whether or not to "give in." Those roles can be reversed, and those roles may also be different for homosexual persons. **Self-image is not enhanced by forcing one's will on another person or by letting oneself be victimized by another person.**

49

Caring relationships with friends of the same sex and the opposite sex can do much to improve our self-images. When we relate honestly to others and are genuinely concerned about them, we are able to give and receive valuable affirmation that almost always results in improved self-images.

All of us find it easier to say NO! to sexual pressure when we learn to say YES! to the best that is within us. Help teens understand that a person who does not want to get to know them at a deep level is not a person who cares enough to ever make a good sexual partner.

9. Help teens consider questions that will guide them in ethical decision-making about sexual activity. Teens need to make their own decisions, but they need help in that process. They also need to have thought about those decisions prior to being in the back seat of a car, in a hotel room, or in a bedroom in one of their homes. In addition to sharing your own values and beliefs, you can make a significant contribution by helping them think about important questions related to their decisions. Here are some questions that are shared in *The Gift of Sexuality* on pages 64–66 concerning decision-making about intercourse:

- Do you want to wait until you are married to have sexual intercourse? How do you feel about intercourse in terms of your relationship with God?

- Do you want to wait until you are older and have had more dating experiences before having sexual intercourse? How do you think intercourse would affect you at this point in your life?

- How do you feel about your communication with the other person? Have you shared your beliefs and values about sexual activity? What else do you need to discuss before intercourse? Have you talked about the past sexual experience you have each had [not necessarily the names of the persons you've been with but what you've done]?

- Have you made adequate arrangements for protection against pregnancy and sexually transmitted disease? If the protection did not work, do you know what you would do in response to a pregnancy or a sexually transmitted disease? Have the two of you talked about that?

- What will sexual intercourse add to your relationship with the other person? Will it really offer anything that you can't have through other ways of expressing physical affection? How important is it to move to intercourse?

- How will having sexual intercourse affect your relationship with God? Have you prayed about this decision?

You'll find other questions raised throughout *The Gift of Sexuality* and also in Part Two of this *Adult Guide*.

Chapter Five:
Homosexuality and Bisexuality

Some national magazines had cover stories in 2005 and 2006 about gay teens in North America. There is a growing recognition that many teens do not have a heterosexual orientation, and our society as a whole is challenged by this realization. As parents, clergy, youth group advisors, and others working with teens, we need to recognize that there are young people in many homes, youth groups, and congregations who are struggling with questions of sexual orientation and may see themselves as other than heterosexual.

When we conducted the *Faith Matters* study, the information we gave to teens who participated included a phone number they could call if they wanted to visit with us about anything in the surveys or about related concerns. Several of those who made calls to us were teens struggling with issues related to sexual orientation. I especially remember my conversation with a teenage female who told me that her father was a member of the church staff, that her church taught that homosexuality was a sin, and that she was convinced she was lesbian. She had contemplated suicide several times but was terrified that ending her life would send her straight to hell. She was convinced that her parents had no idea about her struggle, and she feared that they would kick her out of the home if she told them.

Based on the *Faith Matters* research, the probability is very high that there are homosexual and bisexual teenagers in your congregation. Keep in mind that the *Faith Matters* study involved almost six thousand teenagers from all over the United States, all of whom were active in congregations.

As we have shared the results with clergy and other congregational leaders, most have been surprised by the percentage of teens who didn't have a heterosexual orientation. These figures reflect self-identification of orientation, not behavior. The fact that a person feels he or she has a homosexual orientation does not necessarily mean that person has actually participated in a homosexual act.

	Males	Females
Heterosexual	86%	89%
Homosexual	7%	5%
Bisexual	5%	4%
Don't know	2%	2%

In looking at the results, it's important to be aware that forming a sexual identity or orientation is something that happens during the adolescent years. Some sexuality researchers report that as many as 25% of twelve year olds are unsure of their sexual orientation but that only 5% of eighteen year olds have that same uncertainty. People may be unclear at the start of adolescence about their sexual orientation, but they are usually not unclear by the end of that developmental time.

The American Psychological Association says that sexual orientation is "an enduring emotional, romantic, sexual, or affectional attraction to another person . . . sexual orientation exists along a continuum that ranges from exclusive homosexuality to exclusive heterosexuality and includes various forms of bisexuality." Persons of homosexual orientation have a primary sexual attraction to the same sex in contrast to persons of heterosexual orientation who have a primary sexual attraction to the opposite sex. Bisexual persons are sexually attracted to both the same sex and the opposite sex.

The majority of these teens are leading lives that are in large part secret as far as the congregation is concerned. Eighty-eight percent of the teens who self-identified as homosexual or bisexual indicated that their pastor or rabbi was not aware of their orientation. Only 36% indicated that there was a youth worker, advisor, or other adult leader (besides a parent) in the church who was aware of their orientation.

Eighty-three percent indicated that there was at least one other young person in the congregation who was aware of their orientation, so they are not completely isolated; but only 16% said that the whole youth group or class knew about it. Very few of them have felt sufficiently comfortable to "come out" to their entire youth group or class.

Almost half of these youth (46%) said that their parents were not aware of their sexual orientation or of their struggle over identifying their sexual orientation. I was deeply concerned as I went through survey responses and interviewed teens of homosexual or bisexual orientation to discover how many of them are leading secret lives—at least in their homes and in their congregations. Sexual orientation is a basic part of our identity, and it is a significant problem when teens are not able to comfortably talk about such concerns with their parents and in their youth groups or classes.

Nonheterosexual teens in our study were almost twice as likely as heterosexual teens to have seriously considered suicide. This should be a matter of great concern for those of us who care about youth. The secrecy with which many of these teens feel they must live has to contribute to depression and the feeling that life is not worth living.

Homosexuality and Scripture

There are substantial numbers of persons in North America who see themselves as homosexual or bisexual in their orientation. It is clear to me from reading the comments of teens and from interviewing teens with a nonheterosexual orientation that they are not *choosing* that orientation. While there are still things that we do not know about the factors that contribute to a particular sexual orientation, scientific studies increasingly show that biology plays a role in that process. With the creation story in Genesis and other passages of Scripture affirming the goodness of creation, I find it difficult to condemn homosexuality.

But how does a person reconcile an accepting attitude toward homosexuality with some of the biblical passages that seem to say that homosexual behavior is a sin? If you read some of those passages without considering the context, it does appear that Scripture says homosexuality is a sin.

There was no concept of homosexuality in biblical times as we understand it today. These were condemnations of sexual behavior between men, perhaps in reaction to the use of men and women as sacred prostitutes in nearby religious cults. Let's take a closer look. I'm going to be repeating here some of the same material shared in Chapter Eight of *The Gift of Sexuality*, but I think it is crucial for those of us who work with teens to have a better understanding of what Scripture does and does not say.

First, let's consider the context of the passages most often quoted to show that homosexuality is a sin:

Genesis 19:1–11 really is an account of abuse and assault rather than an attack on homosexuality. It's distressing that the men of the city of Sodom wanted to rape the guests of Lot, and it is just as distressing that Lot offered his two virgin daughters for rape.

Leviticus 18:22; Leviticus 20:13; and **Deuteronomy 23:17–18** are part of what was called the "purity code" in Old Testament times. That same code also prohibits sex with a woman who is menstruating. Other passages in these Old Testament books require styles of dress that we no longer follow. People are also told to stone disobedient children! We do not, fortunately, put equal weight on every instruction found in Leviticus and Deuteronomy. Thus we should not automatically assume that the prohibition of male same-sex behaviors given here should be applied to life today.

1 Corinthians 6:9 has an uncertain meaning, and it depends on the translation used. The New International Version translates a word as "homosexual" that the New Revised Standard Version translates as "male prostitutes."

Romans 1:26–27 seems one of the clearest New Testament prohibitions on homosexual behavior. Some biblical scholars, however, have pointed out that Paul is not speaking here about those born with a homosexual orientation. He seems to be speaking about persons who are heterosexual but are acting as homosexuals—against their own orientation.

1 Timothy 1:10–11 may well have been condemning not homosexuality but pederasty, according to many biblical scholars. Pederasty was the practice of male teachers exploiting their position with male students by requiring them to have sexual relations with them. Thus these were not consensual acts and involved adults with children. In our own time, we would condemn such acts whether they were homosexual or heterosexual.

Second, with all of the passages just identified, it's important to remember that life was very short in biblical times. People were married at a very young age and had as many children as possible. Mary may have been as young as fifteen or sixteen when she gave birth to Jesus. With many people not living far into their thirties, family size was very important. In that kind of culture, it's understandable that homosexual behavior would have been discouraged.

The fact that it may have been discouraged does not necessarily mean that it is a sin. There are biblical passages that urge celibacy (not having sex at all), prohibit divorce, or expect women to be subservient to men. We do not consider those passages authoritative today. Why should we give stronger weight to the very small number of passages that talk about homosexual behavior, especially given the context of those passages?

This seems especially true since Jesus doesn't mention same-sex behavior in the gospels at all. Jesus never felt a need to reference homosexual behavior or to prohibit it. If it were a sin, why is Jesus silent on the topic?

Third, the Bible talks about the friendship of David and Jonathan, and some feel this could have been a homosexual relationship, especially because of 1 Samuel 18:1, which says: "When David had finished speaking to Saul, the soul of Jonathan was bound to the soul of David, and Jonathan loved him as his own soul." There is a Hebrew word that can be translated as "to gird, join, bind, or cling," which could imply a homosexual connection between them. 1 Samuel 20:41 talks about their kissing each other, but that action does not itself make a homosexual relationship. The truth is that we simply do not know with certainty what the passages mean. It is certainly true that the Hebrew Bible or Old Testament celebrates the strong friendship that David and Jonathan had.

Fourth, while there are a small number of passages that are taken by some as condemning homosexual behavior, there are a much larger number of passages that urge us to:

- Show love and acceptance of others in all our relationships.

- Work for justice for all people and care about those who are looked down on by others. Jesus reached out to the poor, to the hated tax collectors, to prostitutes, and to others not cared about by society.

- Forgive persons who behave in ways that are not acceptable. Condemnation is never the last word with God. Jesus urges us in fact not to focus so much on the misbehavior of others as on our own sins and shortcomings. For example, consider the passage in which Jesus tells people not to be focused on the speck or splinter in someone else's eye but on the log in their own [Matthew 7:1–5].

One of the best known teachings of Jesus is often called the Golden Rule and is part of the Great Commandment:

> **You shall love the Lord your God with all your heart and with all your soul, and with all your mind; and your neighbor as yourself.**
> **Luke 10:27**

Then Jesus proceeds to define who our neighbors are by telling the parable of the Good Samaritan, which in fact reminds us that all people are our neighbors (see Luke 10:25–37 for the full parable).

No one has any doubt that this is a commandment that applies to all of our lives. Those of us with a heterosexual orientation should ask ourselves how we would want to be treated if we had a homosexual orientation. We would want to be accepted and affirmed, as it seems clear to me Jesus would have done.

Misconceptions about Homosexuality

As I've visited with clergy, youth workers, parents, and teens around North America, I've become increasingly aware that there are several misconceptions about homosexuality:

1. "Homosexuals are at the root of the AIDS epidemic and are the ones spreading the disease." The sad truth is that HIV/AIDS does not discriminate: it attacks people of all sexual orientations, and it is spread by people of all sexual orientations. Increasing numbers of heterosexual people have HIV/ AIDS, and the *Faith Matters* study makes it clear that ignorance of how to prevent HIV/AIDS is a major problem among teenagers of all orientations. Fifty-five percent of the teens in that study, for example, think that a person cannot get HIV from oral sex.

2. "There really are very few people who are gay, and those persons are trying to have too big an impact on our society with demands for rights." As the *Faith Matters* study clearly shows, a little over ten percent of teens in churches have a nonheterosexual orientation. That is not a small percentage. Moreover, 96% of the teens who completed surveys indicate that they know at least one person their age who has a gay, lesbian, or bisexual orientation. This is a part of life for teenagers today. Secular studies show significant numbers of gay, lesbian, and bisexual adults in society. It should be no surprise to us that young people as well as many adults are concerned about the rights of people who are not heterosexual.

3. "Homosexual adults are a danger to teenagers and children." The truth is that heterosexual adults are more likely to sexually take advantage of teenagers and children than homosexual adults are to do so. Most of the cases of sexual abuse of children involve heterosexual adults, both in terms of absolute numbers and in terms of percentages.

Homosexual adults are not seeking to "make" children or teens into homosexuals. A gay man shared this perspective:

> *Being homosexual has complicated my life beyond belief. It's caused awkwardness in relationships with my parents, my sister, my coworkers, and the people in my church. There is no way that I would "want" others to have the same orientation that I do. It's too difficult a road. I didn't choose this orientation. It's just how I am. I want to be available to help youth who are struggling with issues of orientation, but I would never knowingly influence someone to make this choice.*

Abuse of children and teens by adults is a very serious problem in North America. I feel strongly that all of our congregations should be much more proactive in working to prevent abuse and to give teens the information they need to avoid being abused. Teens are not, however, in any greater danger from homosexual adults than from heterosexual adults. I especially recommend the book *A Time to Heal* by my colleague Debra Haffner; this book gives excellent guidance to congregations dealing with problems of sexual abuse and shows how congregations can be made safer places for people of all ages.

4. "Homosexuals are undermining the institution of marriage." This argument has especially been made by opponents of marriage equality. I'm heterosexual and privileged to be in a healthy marriage to a wonderful person. The fact that a gay couple wants to make a similar commitment to each other and identify their relationship as a marriage is not a threat to my relationship with my wife. In fact I fail to see how what two other people want to call their relationship has any impact on my relationship with my wife.

There are things that threaten the institution of marriage in North America. Sexual relationships outside of the marriage, too many hours spent at work, financial struggles, arguments over how to raise children, and differences of opinion over how to care for elderly parents all have the capacity to threaten a marriage. The tragic truth is that the divorce rate both in society as a whole and among persons who are active in congregations remains distressingly high. Homosexual people are not contributing to those problems.

I sometimes think that our society has a tendency to portray homosexuality and marriage equality as threats to heterosexual marriage because we would prefer not facing the serious problems that exist in the institution of marriage. I'm reminded sadly of a cartoon showing two men sitting at a bar. One of them says to the other something like this: "I don't understand all this talk about letting gay people get married. I thought they already had enough problems."

Gay Teens and the Congregation

All of our faith-based institutions face a tremendous challenge in deciding how to relate to teens who have a homosexual orientation or who have questions about their orientation. Whatever your personal beliefs on this potentially divisive topic in congregational life, I urge you to remember that those of homosexual orientation remain the children of God. I appreciated the words of this Missouri Synod Lutheran pastor, whose denomination definitely considers homosexual behavior a sin:

> *I never thought before about the possibility that we actually had homosexual teenagers who were active in our church. But with a youth group with forty kids in it, we have to have some who are homosexual or at least who are struggling with identity issues. As negative as I've been about homosexuality, none of them would ever approach me. That has to change. We've got to find some more compassionate ways to respond to these young people.*

Homosexuality is a topic about which people of equally strong faith are not always in agreement. Many denominations have continuing internal debate about whether or not homosexuality is a sin and about issues of membership, ordination, and marriage for persons of homosexual orientation or behavior. Some long-time members of faith communities have changed to different religious traditions because of denominational or congregational positions on homosexuality.

When we reviewed sexuality education literature from many denominational traditions as part of the *Faith Matters* study, we observed that:

- There are denominations in which homosexuality is accepted as fully as heterosexuality and in no way viewed as a sin. Those traditions reflect that in their resources, and these denominations practice full inclusion of homosexual persons and ordain or license homosexual persons as clergy.

- There are denominations in which the official position is that homosexuality is a sin but in which a distinction is made between those of homosexual orientation and of homosexual behavior. Acceptance is extended to those of homosexual orientation who are celibate but not to those who are actively involved in a homosexual relationship.

- There are denominations in which homosexuality is viewed as a sin and in which there is a firm belief that people of that orientation can be converted or changed to a heterosexual orientation. Leaders in these traditions are fond of saying, "Hate the sin but love the sinner."

- There are denominations in which the existing sexuality education resources reflect the kind of confusion and conflict over the issue that is present in the denomination. For example, some of those resources speak about the importance of accepting persons of homosexual orientation and maintain that such orientation is not simply a matter of "choice." Homosexuality is not seen as a barrier to membership. But those same traditions then talk about it being impossible to be homosexual and be ordained. If the orientation and behavior are not sinful, why prohibit ordination?

In virtually all of the religious sexuality education resources that we reviewed, with the exception of the first category above, the discussion seems to assume that homosexual persons are not active in the youth class or group—they are outside in the community. Thus even materials that are very accepting of homosexuality as an orientation often appear to take it for granted that there are no young people of homosexual orientation participating in the study. (The *Our Whole Lives* curriculum from the Unitarian Universalist Association and the United Church Board for Homeland Ministries is an exception.)

Those youth who are nonheterosexual and who have a clergy person, youth group advisor, or youth group who are open and nonjudgmental are far more likely to be open within the faith-based community about their orientation. Those who were able to be open in their faith-based communities were also less likely to have considered suicide than other nonheterosexual teens in this study. Those who are in congregations where there are negative views toward homosexuality and bisexuality rarely are open about their orientation. Those teens live with a very painful silence.

A pastor in the United Methodist Church shared a very interesting perspective:

Think about what it says that there are so many kids in our churches who are gay and who aren't open about it. If I were gay and felt disapproval from the church, I'd stop coming. But most of these young people are continuing to be active. That says to me that God and the church are very important to them.

Few issues are as potentially divisive in faith communities as the matter of homosexual orientation and behavior. While some denominations are clearly accepting and others clearly in opposition to homosexuality and bisexuality as orientation and/or behavior, there are many others which are in continuing struggle over the issue. Official denominational positions are not always representative of what clergy and laity within the denominations believe, feel, and think. Here are some concerns that I and the others involved in the *Faith Matters* study share:

- It is very important for congregations to recognize that almost all have at least some youth who are struggling with issues of sexual orientation. As sermons are preached, classes taught, and youth discussions directed, clergy and other leaders need to recognize the high probability that some of the youth participating see themselves as having a nonheterosexual orientation. Not recognizing that reality means that many hurtful comments can be made and increases the probability that these youth will not seek help from their faith-based institution. **Remember, nonheterosexual teens in our study were almost twice as likely as heterosexual teens to have seriously considered suicide.**

- Both parents and teens have a strong need for safe places that these issues can be discussed. Faith-based institutions have the potential to provide those opportunities. It's time to break the silence on this issue in our work with youth. Sexual orientation and related issues need to be openly discussed as part of the congregation's youth program.

- Persons in traditions which continue to feel that homosexuality and bisexuality are abnormal or sinful need to be careful that those issues do not assume more importance than they should. One Missouri Synod Lutheran pastor shared the observation that: "Homosexuality is not the unforgivable sin. Living in a time where people die of hunger, where children and spouses are abused, and where violence has become commonplace in society, we need to keep some perspective."

• Persons in traditions which are accepting of homo-sexuality as an orientation and a behavior have the opportunity for significant ministries not only to their own youth but also to youth in the community who struggle with these issues.

• Adult leaders in all faith-based institutions need to recognize that religious faith and congregational involvement are very important to the youth of nonheterosexual orientation who participated in this study. Whatever the congregation's theological position on these issues, these youth need to experience love and acceptance.

Perspectives for Parents

I hope that the discussion in Chapter Eight of *The Gift of Sexuality* and the material in this chapter of the *Adult Guide* have provided some perspective that is helpful to those of you reading this book who are parents of children or teenagers. I want to offer just a few additional perspectives:

1. If you have a son or daughter struggling with questions of sexual orientation, do not make the mistake of thinking this represents some failure on your part. As I've shared both in this chapter and in the youth book, we still do not know what "causes" a person to be homosexual or bisexual. Growing evidence shows that there is likely a very strong biological cause with perhaps some additional contributions from the environment. There is nothing that you as a parent have done or have not done that has caused your child to have a particular sexual orientation.

2. Even if you are inclined to disapprove of homo-sexuality as an orientation or behavior, be conscious of what you say on the topic to your son or daughter. If your son or daughter does turn out to have a nonheterosexual orientation and has repeatedly heard condemnation of that orientation or behavior from you, that child is very unlikely to be open with you about the orientation. Let your son or daughter know that you are always open to talking with him or her about anything and that you will always love him or her, no matter what happens.

3. Model tolerance and acceptance in the way that you talk about persons of other sexual orientations. Your son or daughter will be more influenced by your values than by the values of anyone else. If you model tolerance and acceptance, your son or daughter is far more likely to do the same. Your son or daughter is living in a world in which an increasing number of persons are open about having a nonheterosexual orientation. Our society is healthier and our relationships are healthier when we have tolerance and indeed acceptance of persons who are different from us. Be a part of making the world a better place, and encourage your son or daughter to do the same.

4. Take advantage of opportunities to talk with your son or daughter about sexual orientation and behavior. Comments from your teenager about things that happened at school, movies, television programs, popular music, newspapers, and magazines frequently raise issues of orientation and behavior. Use these as opportunities for dialogue with your son or daughter. Your own openness will make it more likely that your son or daughter will be open with you.

5. Remember that the years between twelve and eighteen are a time when sexual identity is being fully formed. The fact that a twelve or thirteen year old has some homosexual feelings does not absolutely mean that he or she will end up with a homosexual orientation. Creating an environment in which your son or daughter can talk about questions of orientation results in greater health for your child and for your relationship with your child.

There is, in my opinion, nothing wrong with a homosexual orientation. The majority of people in our culture, however, do have a heterosexual orientation. Adolescence is the time in which that orientation gets identified for most people, and it can take a few years for some teens to complete that process.

6. Be concerned about the justice issues for homosexuals and other sexual minorities such as bisexuals and transgender persons. We should be strongly opposed to:

- Unkind and sometimes violent treatment of sexual minorities.

- Ridicule or jokes made at the expense of sexual minorities.

- Hiring practices and employment policies which discriminate against sexual minorities.

- Laws which discriminate against sexual minorities.

- Attitudes of hate and prejudice toward sexual minorities.

7. Get help for yourself and your son or daughter. Find a PFLAG (Parents and Friends of Lesbians and Gays) group in your area. Find out if there is a group in your denomination working on behalf of the rights of homosexual persons. Contact some of the organizations listed in the "Resources" section of this book, such as Advocates for Youth.

More to Consider

There are limitations of space, but I want to encourage you to learn more about:

- Those persons who are described as transsexual or transgender. Pages 115–116 of *The Gift of Sexuality* provide background about this.

- The growing movement for marriage equality, granting to gay and lesbian couples the same rituals and the same rights as heterosexual couples enjoy. If you have not thought seriously about this issue, the possibility may make you uncomfortable. A full discussion of this goes beyond the scope of this book, but I urge you to keep an open mind and to become better informed on the topic. The Religious Institute on Sexual Morality, Justice, and Healing has an informative "Open Letter on Marriage Equality," which you can find at their website listed in the "Resources" section of this book.

Chapter Six:
Dating and Love

The word *dating* does not mean the same thing to all young people, and some young people are not using the word at all. Commonly used substitutions include *going out* and *seeing.* Your community may have other variations. Whatever the terminology used, young people are intensely interested in going out with others; and these relationships become an extremely high priority for almost all teenagers. Some of the most difficult decisions parents of teenagers face concern these relationships:

- At what age should I permit my son or daughter to begin dating?

- How many nights a week should I let my son or daughter go out?

- How much financial support should I contribute to the social life of my son or daughter?

- How much freedom should I give my son or daughter to entertain in our home?

- How much should I be influenced by what other parents permit?

- How much should I be concerned about knowing the background of the people my son or daughter sees?

- What kind of curfew should I set for dating on school nights, on weekends, and on special occasion nights?

- What kinds of punishment or consequences are appropriate for violation of rules related to dating?

- Should I permit my son or daughter to "go steady," that is to go out with only one person?

• Should I permit my son or daughter to go out with someone who is considerably older or considerably younger?

And so the list continues! These are very important decisions because they have great impact on the well-being of teenagers and also on the relationship between teens and their parents.

As adults, we are often guilty of taking lightly the romantic feelings of young people—especially of junior high youth. If we show that we do not take their feelings seriously, we guarantee that they will not take our advice or counsel seriously. Parents and others working with youth need to recognize that feelings are real—not only for young people but for adults as well. We may approve or disapprove of the way that a teenager feels, but the feeling is valid for the young person and should be taken seriously by us.

Both adults and teens, of course, also need to recognize that we do not have to permit our feelings to control our decisions or define our identity. A person can *feel* strongly attracted to another person without acting on that feeling each time it is experienced. It's perfectly possible to feel attracted to a person whom we recognize, when we think about it, is probably not a good match for us. The fact that we *feel* angry about something that has happened to us does not mean that our identity has to become that of an angry person. Feelings are real and powerful, but they do not have to control our lives.

Being in Love

What does it mean to be "in love"? The experience of being in love is one which young people should be encouraged to talk about, and adults should accept the validity of those feelings (even though recognizing that these feelings will change with the passage of time). The kind of initial attraction and infatuation that teens experience, of course, is only one type of love.

It's important for teens to understand that the love rooted in this infatuation is not a good model for a healthy, life-long relationship. With teen novels, movies, and television shows primarily focused on strongly passionate, initial attraction and on sexual desire, it's no wonder that many teens come to see that as the only kind of love between two people. We should not be dismissive of this kind of love because it is very real. If we think back to our own teenage years, we can remember how significant and important to our lives those first experiences of "falling in love" and "being in love" were to us. We need to extend the same respect to our teens that we wanted to receive from adults when we were teenagers. We also need to be prepared to help teens understand the complexity of love and relationships.

Helen Fisher of Rutgers University has done extensive research, on the basis of which she has proposed that we fall in love in three stages:

- Lust
- Attraction or romantic love
- Attachment

Through brain scans and biochemical research on people in love, scientists have learned that each of those stages corresponds to a different part of the brain and to different chemicals. Our biochemistry really does have a great deal to do with the way that we experience attraction and love. Here's some more background on the three stages:

Lust is driven by the hormones testosterone and estrogen. Lust drives our attraction to other people and is rooted in the biological drive to achieve sexual gratification and to reproduce. People who acted on all their feelings of lust, of course, would be exhausted and lacking in the benefits of a long-term, committed relationship.

Attraction or romantic love is what causes us to choose a single person out of the many potential partners in the world. The chemicals dopamine, norepinephrine and serotonin all play a role in this stage. This is sometimes called the "love struck" phase because people in this phase have difficulty thinking about anything else! Some people have less appetite and even need less sleep than usual. There is a great tendency in this stage to focus rather obsessively on the romantic relationship with other matters feeling much less important by comparison. People in this stage do not always make the best students or employees—they have more energy but they also place less importance on work! They tend to feel delighted with their lives and happier than they had thought possible. This kind of love, however, only lasts between seven and eighteen months.

The attachment phase is crucial for any long-term relationship. There are two hormones released by the nervous system that are thought to contribute to the attachment phase. Oxytocin is released by both men and women during orgasm and is thought to promote bonding and to contribute to the pleasant sense of well-being and peace that follows orgasm. (It is also released by the hypothalamus during childbirth and helps deepen the bond between mother and child). Vasopressin also plays a role in long-term relationships. This phase is one of greater peace and security than the romantic love stage. While biochemistry plays a role, this stage is rooted in the commitment that we make to another person and in our willingness to honor that commitment through the ups and the downs of life.

Thinking about this in more spiritual terms, one can say that lust is the reminder that God intends for us to have pleasure in sexual relationships; romantic love reminds us that we were created with a drive to share life with another person in a way that is different than all other relationships; and attachment brings the reality that security and peace are only possible when we are willing to make deep commitments to God and to each other.

Some people get blocked at the level of lust and have difficulty even moving on to romantic love. Many people find themselves disillusioned when romantic love begins to fade and end up searching for a new romantic love rather than moving to the stage of attachment. And some people make the initial move to the attachment phase without a willingness to do the hard work that is required for a long-term relationship to work. My colleague Debra Haffner shares these very wise words:

> "We can do a better job of helping people from a very young age understand that it is expected that romantic love fades. You remember the fairy tale ending: 'they fell in love, they got married, and—they lived happily ever after.' When I would read those stories to my children, I would change the ending: 'they fell in love, they got married, and—it was a lot of work.'"

The Gift of Sexuality talks not only about dating and sexuality but also about marriage and parenting. Teens need to see that throughout the dating or relationship-building process they are gaining the experiences that will help them make good marriage choices and that will prepare them to be healthy marriage partners and healthy parents. They need to recognize that all of these experiences connect to the spiritual life.

Love in the Scriptures, of course, goes beyond the romantic love of one person for another. Both the Hebrew Bible and the New Testament teach us to love our neighbors as ourselves and to care about the needs of the world. The love between two persons in a committed relationship and the love between a person and God can provide the framework for a life that is committed to the needs of others. We should desire for our children a life that is filled with love for God, for one's mate, for the rest of one's family, and for those in the world in which we have been placed. We should model that kind of love in our own lives.

Thoughts for Parents on Teens and Dating

Youth often ask permission to date or go out with another person at a particular age or under particular circumstances on the basis that:

- "Kathy's parents let her do it."

- "Tom's father doesn't care what time he comes in."

- "Everyone else gets to do it."

- "If I don't go, I'll be the only one in the whole school."

Adults obviously recognize that *everyone* rarely agrees on *anything.* Many parents understandably resent being told they should permit something simply because some other parent permits it.

At the same time, one cannot totally ignore local community norms and customs. If most young people are permitted to start dating as freshman in high school in your community, then you may be putting a social stigma on a son or daughter if you refuse to permit any dating until the senior year. Making a son or daughter appear overly different from others sometimes invites outright rebellion at a later age. At the same time, community norms very often result in young people beginning dating activity at too early an age. What should you do? You want to be aware of community norms, but ultimately you want to make the decision that you know is best for the teenager you love.

It's also important to recognize that you may be able to control whether or not you let a son or daughter go out with another teen, but you can't control what his or her feelings are for someone else. Many young people start having boyfriends and girlfriends during the middle school/junior high years. You may or may not feel comfortable about that as a parent, but you can't prevent them from establishing that relationship.

Every situation is different because of the uniqueness of the teens with whom you live or work and the uniqueness of community in which you live. The following guidelines may be relevant for clergy and youth workers but are especially intended for parents. The "guidelines" are just that; they are not all-inclusive, always-applicable rules.

First, do everything possible to encourage a teenage son or daughter to talk about his or her romantic feelings and social experiences. Try to be open, accepting, and affirming. Don't overreact, and don't offer too much advice. If you are genuinely open, listen carefully, and show your concern, your son or daughter will seek your advice. Remember—it is far better to be told things with which you disagree than not to have communication. If teenagers find that their parents always react with criticism of what they have done, they quickly learn to be secretive about their activities.

Second, try to have some awareness of what other teenagers are doing and not doing as far as dating is concerned. This doesn't mean that you should permit what others permit. It does mean that you can do a better job making decisions and guiding your own teenager if you have some idea what common practice in the community actually is.

Third, in general, discourage one-to-one middle school/ junior high dating. Group social activities are all right for junior highs. School events and church or synagogue events offer good opportunities for group contact with members of the opposite sex and should be encouraged.

If you choose to permit your middle school/junior high son or daughter to go out with another person on a date that is not part of a group activity, be sure that you do not let them be in a situation where they are tempted to be involved in sexual activity for which they are not emotionally prepared. By virtue of the fact that middle school/junior high young people do not have licenses to drive, parents retain some significant control over where they go and over what they do. You don't want to convey distrust of your son or daughter; you simply want to use caution. And you want to speak frankly about your values concerning what they do and do not do when together with another person.

Fourth, discourage significant age differences between your son or daughter and the person your son or daughter dates. The statistics about sexual activity and expectations make it clear that younger females dating older males are going to be under a great deal of pressure. Junior high girls should not date high school boys, and high school girls should not date post-high boys. In those instances one must face not only the age difference but also the life experience difference.

In general, it is best if there is not more than a two-year age difference between the two people going out together. And, of course, there are exceptions to all the preceding statements. An extremely mature high school girl may be fine dating a sensitive and non-manipulative post-high boy. Many teenagers, however, are not as mature or as sensitive as they like to feel they are. For that matter, the same is true for a good many of us as adults.

Fifth, make it clear that you do expect to be introduced to the friends of your son or daughter and that you want to get acquainted with them. You certainly do not want your son or daughter going out with someone you know nothing about at all. Seek opportunities to meet their friends, both male and female. Create an open atmosphere in your home that encourages your son or daughter to talk about their friends. Tell them you want to know if they have a boyfriend or a girlfriend, and ask them about that person. Be genuine in your interest and very, very slow to criticize the choice your son or daughter has made.

Sixth, encourage your offspring to entertain in your home. Part of the strong middle school/junior high desire to date can be compensated for by letting your son or daughter have a friend of the opposite sex over to do homework together or share a soft drink or work on a school project. If that kind of pattern is established early, that same son or daughter will probably continue to entertain in your home. You have for more control; they are exposed to far less temptation; and you have a better opportunity to become personally acquainted with their friends.

Older teens have an increasing desire for privacy when with members of the opposite sex. Many parents have heard horror stories of drinking parties while parents were gone, and of teenagers sharing in sexual intercourse in the master bedroom while the parents were out for supper. While those situations are certainly to be avoided, you should extend some privacy to older teens. After all, if they cannot have some privacy in your home, they will find privacy in other places! The very fact that they are in your home places some inhibitions on their behavior.

Providing privacy in your home can take many forms. At one level, it may be letting them entertain in the living room, family room, or kitchen while you are present in another room. If you have great confidence in your son or daughter, you may come to feel comfortable with being out of the house for a short time when they are entertaining members of the opposite sex. If you have a high school senior, you should be aware that he or she is only a short time away from graduation and living on his or her own—in an apartment or a college dormitory. If you cannot begin to trust them in your own home alone, what magical transformation do you expect to take place in their responsibility level when they leave home?

Seventh, work yourself out of the job of being decision-maker and disciplinarian for your son or daughter. As teenagers move from the seventh grade through graduation from high school, they should be having increasing freedom to make their own decisions—including the right to live with the consequences of some wrong decisions.

When teenagers date, parents obviously need to know whom their son or daughter is with, where they are going, and when they will be back. Parents should also provide good models by keeping their children informed of their own plans. Safety and common sense indicate that this information should be shared by all members of the household. If you are open about what you are doing, your son or daughter will be more willing to show the same kind of openness.

Rather than arbitrarily informing your son or daughter about your rules concerning their going out with someone, try involving them in conversation with you about what are reasonable expectations. See if you can agree together on the guidelines for their behavior. You may also want to determine with your son or daughter what the consequences should be for not keeping the covenant that you've made together. When teens are a part of setting their own guidelines, they are much more likely to follow them and also much less likely to be resentful of any consequences for their failure to do so. Remember that you want to be less and less a rule enforcer and more and more an advisor as your son or daughter matures.

A sample covenant by a high school junior named Ashley (an only child) and her parents follows. She and her parents talked about the covenant at a focus group during the *Faith Matters* study. While it was written out by the mother, it's based on a discussion the three of them had together.

Ashley, interestingly, was the one who pushed for the nights before classes to be reserved more for the family and for study. She took her schoolwork very seriously and wanted to have a ready response when pressured by friends to do activities that would interfere with that work. She also was frustrated that her father was in a pattern of working at his office through supper so many nights of the week, and both she and her mother encouraged him in the conversation to start coming home earlier to share supper or go out for supper together even if he had to do more work later. Here's the agreement, which they posted on the refrigerator:

1. Nights before Ashley's classes (Sunday after youth group, Monday, Tuesday, Wednesday, and Thursday) are for family time, study, and school activities. We'll eat at home together as often as we can, and all three of us will make a significant effort to do so. These aren't dating nights, but Ashley's friends, including her boyfriend, are always welcome to join us for supper. She's also welcome to have friends over to study and watch television. If any of the three of us won't be home for supper because we have something else to do, we'll try our best to tell the others by breakfast so we all know how to plan. We'll all try really hard to keep Wednesday night free for supper together even when the other nights get busy.

2. Friday and Saturday nights are both times when it's fine for Ashley to go out with her boyfriend or with other friends. She'll always let Mom and Dad know who she'll be with, where they are going, and when she'll be home. It isn't all right to stay out later than the state-imposed curfew of midnight unless a parent is along. If something comes up to change plans, Ashley promises to call Mom and Dad to let them know what's happened.

3. The daytime on Saturday gets used for whatever things we put on the calendar. When the three of us agree that there's something we're going to do together, then we all work to honor that commitment.

4. Sunday morning is reserved for church, and Sunday evening is for youth group at church for Ashley. We'll try to have a late supper together on Sunday, unless youth group is sharing a meal. Sunday afternoon is like Saturday during the day.

5. If Mom or Dad isn't home, it's still fine for Ashley to have friends over. The liquor cabinet is always off limits, and she agrees not to be in a bedroom with her boyfriend if no parent is at home unless permission has been given.

6. Ashley agrees to avoid alcohol, illegal drugs, unprotected sex, and anything else that would make Mom and Dad crazy. If Ashley ever is in a difficult situation, a call on the cell will bring Mom or Dad to get her with no questions asked.

7. All three of us promise to be honest with each other about what we are doing and about who we are doing it with. Ashley has always been trustworthy, and we don't see a reason to give penalties or consequences for not keeping this covenant. If the covenant isn't kept, then we'll have to renegotiate everything. And Dad being home for supper more often is part of the covenant.

All three of them signed the covenant. Because of the maturity with which Ashley had always acted, it didn't feel right to her mother or father to determine consequences if she violated her part of the covenant. Her parents felt it very unlikely that she would do that, and they also believed that the knowledge she had betrayed their confidence would be worse

75

than any punishment they would give. If her reliability and honesty changed, then they would renegotiate the covenant.

A similar covenant was made between a boy named Joel and both of his parents and stepparents. There had been problems in consistency between the two households between which he divided his time, and there also had been instances of unreliability on his part. He suggested for that covenant what the consequences should be if he did not keep the agreement, including: loss of use of the car for a month if he came home drunk; being grounded for a weekend if he came home late or lied about where he was going; and being grounded for a month if there was a second offense.

Eighth, it's also crucial, as shared throughout this book, to provide your teens with the information that they need to make the best possible decisions about sexual activity. If they have accurate information and have been encouraged to consider the spiritual dimension of their sexuality, they are far more likely to make mature, healthy decisions.

Ninth, have faith that you have done a good job raising your son or daughter. As young people enter high school, the ability of parents to control their behavior declines rapidly. That doesn't have to be a strong concern. If you have done a good job preparing them to make decisions and have helped them develop confidence in themselves, you do not need to be afraid of the decisions that they make. If you show them that you trust them and have confidence in them, they are far more likely to seek your help and advice. Good communication and mutual respect is worth far more than the limited control that you can exercise.

Tenth, have faith that God will help provide direction and understanding to you and your children. When we live with openness to God's activity in our lives, we generally receive the help and reassurance that are important to us. Prayer can be part of our daily lives, and we can also encourage teens to make it part of their lives. The more we as parents model that time for devotions, prayer, and congregational life are important to us, the more likely it is that our sons and daughters will come to share the same values and practices.

Part Two:
Discussion Guide to
The Gift of Sexuality

Suggestions for Use in the Home

There's a good possibility, if you are a parent reading this book, that you've already given *The Gift of Sexuality* to your son or daughter. Direct reading by teenagers is the purpose for which the book was intended.

Chapter Two of this *Guide* on "Talking about Sexuality" focused on strategies to make it more comfortable to visit with your son or daughter about sexuality concerns. Here are a few additional thoughts that may be helpful to you:

- If you have not already done so, be sure to read *The Gift of Sexuality* yourself so that you have the same information that your son or daughter does. Many of us as adults are not as current as we should be on topics like contraception, HIV, and other sexually transmitted diseases. We also may not have carefully considered how much the Bible does (and does not) have to say on the topic of sexuality and relationships.

- *The Gift of Sexuality* invites the reader to respond to a variety of assessments and quizzes. You should consider having two copies of *The Gift of Sexuality* so that you have a copy in which you can write and to which you can refer and so that your son or daughter has one that does not need to be shared with you. If you only want to invest in one copy, the best approach is to read it yourself and make any notes you want before giving it to your son or daughter.

- You can give *The Gift of Sexuality* to your son or daughter, inviting him or her to come to you with any questions or concerns. A better strategy, however, is to take the initiative in asking your son or daughter what thoughts or questions the book raises. You may want to make your own list of possible questions for discussion that occur to you as you read the book.

• You can suggest to your son or daughter that the two of you read the book together. Set a tentative schedule for going through the chapters and for talking about them. In the field-testing of this resource, we found teens going through the book rapidly because of their interest in the subject matter. You may want to schedule discussion of a couple of chapters at a time. The questions and activities that follow in Part Two can provide suggestions to help you in discussion, but you should not go through the book with your son or daughter as though teaching a class. Your approach needs to be much more informal.

• With *The Gift of Sexuality* and this *Guide* as resources, be alert for the continuing opportunities to talk about sexuality and relationships which come through stories in the news media; movies, television, and music; and the questions raised by your son or daughter.

• Encourage your church or synagogue to have a series of classes on *The Gift of Sexuality,* which will provide opportunity for your son or daughter to talk about these concerns with other teens.

Suggestions for Use in Church, Synagogue, or Community Groups

The Gift of Sexuality can be used for study and discussion in a variety of groups in the church, synagogue, or community. For example:

- As a study in a regular Sunday School class or other religious education setting. This *Guide* provides discussion and activity suggestions for up to thirteen sessions, which is a quarter of study in many traditions.

- Use *The Gift of Sexuality* as the basis for a series of sessions in a church youth group or other informal setting. You can go through the book systematically in six, eight, or thirteen weeks; or you can use the chapter topics as the focus for individual youth group sessions throughout the year.

- Have a special class that focuses on the book and is at a time different than other youth classes or groups.

- Use portions of the book as the basis for a retreat or cover the whole book in a series of retreats.

- Use the book as the primary resource for a summer camp.

- Arrange a special study for both youth and adults, in which adults go through the book in their own group at the same time youth are going through the book.

- Use the book as the basis for a community study, working in cooperation with other churches or synagogues and with community organizations.

While it's beneficial to spend thirteen classes or group meetings covering the entire book, you can also shorten the study to six classes or eight classes. You can also pick and choose chapters for individual classes or group meetings scattered through the year if you prefer.

For six classes or group meetings:
    Class or Group Meeting One covering two sessions from this *Guide*:
        Session One, What Is Sexuality?
        Session Two, Health and Appearance
    Class or Group Meeting Two covering two sessions from this *Guide*:
        Session Three, Abstinence and Slowing Things Down
        Session Four, Masturbation, Kissing, and Touching
    Class or Group Meeting Three covering one session from this *Guide*:
        Session Five, Oral Sex and Intercourse
    Class or Group Meeting Four covering one session from this *Guide*:
        Session Six, Homosexuality and Bisexuality
    Class or Group Meeting Five covering one session from this *Guide*:
        Session Seven, The Bible and Religious Beliefs
    Class or Group Meeting Six covering two sessions from this *Guide*:
        Session Eight, Unwanted Sex
        Session Nine, Contraception, Pregnancy, STDs,
           and Abortion

For eight classes or group meetings, add to the above:
    Class or Group Meeting Seven covering one session from this *Guide*:
        Session Ten, A Guide to Dating
    Class or Group Meeting Eight covering two sessions from this *Guide*:
        Session Eleven, A Guide to Marriage
        Session Twelve, A Guide to Parenting

For thirteen classes or group meetings, do all of the sessions in this *Guide*.

    Sessions Five, Six, and Nine cover an especially
    large amount of material. You could spend an
    additional class on any of those. Session Thirteen

is a "wrap-up" session and can be deleted if you need more time to cover other material.

For a retreat setting, consider using three weekends, covering four sessions each of the first two weekends and five sessions the final weekend.

Consider holding an informal meeting for parents or for parents and teens together at the start of the study. That way parents will know what to expect. Some of the material in the first chapter of *The Gift of Sexuality* can provide a focus for such a group.

Some congregations may wish to use a study of *The Gift of Sexuality* as an outreach effort. Use fliers and news releases to alert people in the community to the fact that you are doing this study. Invite interested teens and parents from the community to share in the study process. Have the teens in your youth class or group share invitations with their friends at school. Teens are intensely interested in this subject matter, and they are seeking opportunities to explore these issues from a religious perspective. Many parents of teens know that they should be doing more to help their sons and daughters but are unsure how to proceed. If they know that a church or synagogue is hosting such a study, they may be interested in participating.

For most of the session activities that
follow in this *Guide,* you need little
more than chalkboard or a flip chart;
chalk or markers; pens or pencils;
notecards or slips of paper; and Bibles.
A few of the activities suggest that you
make short film clips on videotape or
DVDs; some require gathering
newspapers or magazines; some
involve preparing a game; and a few
suggest a guest speaker. You will
want to look through each session
plan at least a couple of weeks in
advance to decide on the specific
activities you want to do and to make
any needed arrangements.

A word about media. *Television programs, films, Internet sites, magazines, and music are all media that connect in powerful ways with teens.*

Some of the sessions that follow suggest that you use a film clip from a television show or a movie as part of the session. A "film clip" just means using a short section (3–10 minutes) of the program or movie rather than the entire show. In some instances, you might want to use a couple of minutes from each of two, three, or even four advertisements or programs. Though you may not be familiar with how to edit those clips together, there is a good chance that someone in your youth group knows how to do it and would be happy to do so.

Books have a long shelf life, often ten years or more. Because television programs change so frequently and movies go in-and-out of popularity so quickly, it seemed unwise to recommend specific programs or movies in this book. Doing so would date the book too quickly and would not be useful.

Ask the teens in your group to help you select programs and movies that will be of interest.

One caution: always preview the film clip yourself before showing it to the group!

*These class or group meeting plans can be utilized
with junior or senior high youth. I do not
recommend using these plans with youth younger
than the seventh grade.*

*You will find discussions having a different level of
depth when doing the classes or group meetings
with older youth rather than younger youth.*

*If you can avoid doing so, try not to have a single
class that includes the seventh grade through the
twelfth grade. The life experience differences for
that kind of span are just too great. The best
combinations are 7th and 8th together and 9th thru
12th together OR 7th thru 9th and 10th thru 12th. In
some very large congregations or community
settings, you may be able to have classes or group
meetings separately for each year.*

*The "Resources" section of this **Guide** lists the **Our
Whole Lives** curriculum, which is a comprehensive
curriculum that starts in age-appropriate ways with
K–1.*

Session One
Chapter Three: What Is Sexuality?

By the end of this session, teens should:
- have gained a better understanding of the way that sexuality pervades our culture.
- have gained an understanding that *sexuality is our way of being in the world as male and female* and recognize that it involves much more than specific sexual acts.
- be able to identify some of the major influences on their views of sexuality.

Decide how you want to handle the opening of this session. Making a video or DVD or having newspapers and magazines available will require some additional preparation.

1. Option One: A great way to open this session is by having a video or DVD prepared which shows some images of sexuality from popular television programs and advertisements. You may well have some teens in your church or synagogue who would be glad to help you create a three-to-seven minute tape or DVD of some of those images.

Option Two: An alternative opening activity would be to have several current newspapers and magazines and to invite teens to work in teams of two or three to create collages about sexuality made up of clippings from those publications (pictures glued or taped to posterboard).

Option Three: If preparation time does not permit you to do either of the first two options, then invite teens to help you make a list of some of the ways sexuality is portrayed and used in the media. Put the list on chalkboard or newsprint. The list might include, for example:

- Sex is used to sell automobiles.

- TV couples are always attractive and glamorous.

- Spending money is portrayed as a way to show love.

Whichever option you use, ASK: *Why* do you think sex is used so often in advertising? Why are the people on television shows so often ultra-attractive and glamorous rather than every-day looking? In what ways do the media provide a distorted view of sexuality? Are there things about sexuality that can be learned from the media? Why, or why not?

Point out that in the course of this study, you will be looking together at the relationship between sexuality and religious faith. You may wish to share a copy of the schedule for the study, indicating the chapter and topic that will be covered each week. Share with the teens that they are welcome to read ahead the chapter for each week but that it isn't necessary to have read the chapter in order to participate in the discussion. Tell them that you will be completing some of the exercises that appear in *The Gift of Sexuality* as a part of the class sessions. They can do the exercises in advance if they want, but opportunity will be provided during your class or group time.

2. Provide a few minutes for teens to complete the "What Do You Know?" activity on pages 10–12 of *The Gift of Sexuality*. They should mark an X on each line indicating how character-istic that activity is of them with **7** indicating "very character-istic" and **1** indicating "not at all characteristic."

Don't put individuals on the spot to share their responses to those items. Do invite teens to share any concerns that they are especially interested in being sure to cover during this study. You may want to list those concerns on chalkboard or newsprint and post them somewhere in your meeting room.

3. Have a volunteer read aloud **Genesis 1:27–31**, which talks about our having been created in the image of God. Divide the group into pairs and invite each person to take a turn being a mirror for his or her partner. Have them stand facing each other, and then have one person mimic or reflect the movements made by the other person. You may want to demonstrate this with a volunteer.

Point out that, while each person is reflecting what the other person does, that doesn't make the two persons identical. In the same way, we are made in the image of God but we are certainly not identical to God. Then have the group make their own list of what it means to be in the image of God. Pages 20–21 of *The Gift of Sexuality* provide some helpful examples.

Then go back to the discussion about "What Is Sexuality?" that appears on pages 19–20 of *The Gift of Sexuality*. [Page numbers throughout these session plans will refer to pages in *The Gift of Sexuality* unless otherwise noted.] Give special attention to James Nelson's definition: *Sexuality is our way of being in the world as male and female.* ASK: What does that mean?

4. Have the group create their own list of influences on their sexuality, drawing in part on material in pages 23–29.

Then have teens complete the "Thinking about Your Own View of Sexuality" activity on pages 29–30. When they have had time to complete the list, invite those who are willing to share any observations they have about the influences on their values and beliefs about sexuality.

5. Have volunteers read aloud the statements from teens about their faith and congregational life that appear on pages 26–27. Then close with prayer.

Session Two
Chapter Four: Health and Appearance

By the end of this session, teens should:
- understand that our bodies are a good gift from a loving God and are intended to be a source of pleasure.
- understand some of the changes in our bodies that take place during puberty.
- have given serious consideration to the role that physical appearance should and should not play in how we feel about ourselves and about others.
- have gained some increased understanding of habits to improve our physical health and overall well-being.

An alternative approach to this session would be to have a physican, a nurse, or a sexuality educator present the factual information to the group and be available to answer questions.

1. Give each teen a notecard and a pen or pencil. Have teens respond to the "How I Feel about My Body" exercise on pages 38–39 by writing their responses on the notecard. Tell them not to put their names on the cards.

Then collect the cards, shuffle them, and pass them out again so that each teen is holding a card but not his or her own. Then take hand-counts to see how many persons in the group chose each of the options for the five items. Write the totals on chalkboard or newsprint. Have people raise their hands on the basis of the card they are holding.

ASK: Did any of the responses from the group surprise you? Why, or why not? Why do people place so much importance on physical appearance in our culture? What is the difference between being concerned about appearance and being concerned about health? Is it possible to be very attractive and not especially healthy? Why, or why not? Is it possible to be very healthy and not especially attractive? Why, or why not? What determines "attractiveness" in our culture?

2. Talk about appearance issues in deciding whether or not to go out with someone. With which of the statements from teens on pages 40–41 do teens most agree or most strongly identify? Why?

Then look at the nine "Guidelines on Physical Appearance" on pages 44–45. ASK: Which of the guidelines are most needed by your friends at school? Why? What additional guidelines would you add?

3. Have a volunteer read aloud **1 Corinthians 3:16–17**. ASK: What does it mean to think of your body as the temple of God? What does this say about the importance of taking care of our bodies? If each person's body is a temple of God, what does that suggest about how we should view the bodies of others?

4. Divide into three small groups, and give one of these tasks to each group:

Group One: Make a list of the changes that occur during puberty for males and females based on material in *The Gift of Sexuality* on pages 32–38. Put the list on newsprint so it can be shared with the rest of the group.

Group Two: Make a list of things people can do to improve their physical health, drawing on material on pages 45–50. Put the list on newsprint so it can be shared with the rest of the group.

Group Three: Make a list of the main health concerns that you see among people at the school or schools attended by group members. Put the list on newsprint so it can be shared with the rest of the group.

Then have all three of the small groups make reports.

5. Go around the group, inviting each person to share one thing about his or her health or appearance for which he or she is especially thankful. Then close with prayer.

Session Three
Chapter Five: Abstinence and Slowing Things Down

By the end of this session, teens should:
* be able to share some of the reasons why it is better to take things slowly and to abstain from intercourse.
* have a better understanding of the issues involved in choosing to make a pledge to abstain.
* have thought about their responses to some of the questions that should be considered before intimate sexual activity.

1. Play the "When Should You. . . .?" game. This takes a little advance preparation. The game works best if played in groups or three or four. Decide on the best number of groups. Then make a large game board out of newsprint or posterboard with the categories below for each small group you anticipate having. Another approach is to place a notecard for each category at spaces on a table that the group members sit around.

* At age 12
* At age 16
* At age 18
* At age 21
* When married
* When engaged
* When in love
* On the first date
* On the second date
* On the fifth date
* Never
* Anytime

Then make a set of slips of paper for each group based on the activites listed in the boxes which follow. You may simply want to make photocopies of the page and then cut out the boxes. Also feel free to add additional activities. You can tape the slips of paper onto notecards or write the activities onto notecards if you prefer.

Go on a first date   Have a midnight curfew

Kiss   Have oral sex

Have sexual intercourse   Masturbate

Get a driver's license   Drink alcohol

Smoke tobacco   Use marijuana

Get a first job   Go on group dates

Go to an all night party   Double date

Be able to get birth control without parental approval

Be able to get an abortion without parental approval

Be able to choose a date without parental approval

Be able to get a marriage license

Rent a hotel room   Have a credit card

Stay home alone when parents are out of town

The game is played by going around the small group in a clockwise circle, starting with the person whose birthday is closest to today. The slips of paper or notecards should be shuffled and placed upside down in the center of the table. Each person in turn draws a slip of paper or a card, reads it aloud, and then places it on the category on the board where he or she thinks it belongs. Have that person share why he or she thinks it belongs on that category. Encourage others in the group to respond and discuss (even argue!) about where the card should go.

Another approach: Instead of having people draw slips/cards and place them in front of others, consider giving each person a full set of the slips/cards. Then have people silently walk around placing those slips of cards face down on the categories. Then the group can talk about the total number of responses in each category.

2. After the "When Should You . . .?" game, discuss as a total group:

- Why was it difficult to decide where to put some of the cards? Why was there so much (or so little) disagreement?

- How did you feel when it was your turn? Were you afraid of what the other people in the group would think of your choices?

- Are decisions in real life as simple and "boxed in" as they were represented in this game? Why, or why not? What makes real life so complicated? Why do some people think there are definite, absolute answers to questions like these?

3. Talk about the popularity of pledges as a means of slowing down sexual activity. Summarize the material on pages 52–55, giving special attention to the five bullets on pages 54–55 on things to keep in mind in making a pledge. ASK: Why are pledges so popular with adults? What are the advantages of making an abstinence pledge? What are the risks of making such a pledge?

4. Talk about the six points on pages 57–63. Present a summary to the group yourself, or assign two of the points to

each of three small groups, and invite the groups to make a report or share a summary. As a total group, make a list of factors that push people toward early sexual experiences.

5. Look at **Luke 10:25–37** which contains the parable of the Good Samaritan. What does the concern for the well-being of others suggest about the nature of our sexual relationships? How does the parable of the Good Samaritan relate to the "Decision-Making Questions" that appear on pages 64–66?

Session Four
Chapter Six: Masturbation, Kissing, and Touching

By the end of this session, teens should:
- have gained an understanding of the reality that masturbation is a normal activity, which most people do but do not talk about doing.
- have a better understanding of how other teens feel about the kissing and touching activities in which they have participated.
- have thought through how they view these activities relative to their own lives.

Be careful not to put teens under pressure to talk about what they have or have not personally done as you go through this session and the one that follows. The questions provided have been worded to be as comfortable as possible, but don't be concerned if you do not get response to some of them. You may need to take more of the lead in discussion for these two sessions.

An additional or alternative activity for this session would be to make a film clip on DVD or video of kissing scenes from movies or television programs. Use that as an introduction to the session or to activity #5.

1. Summarize the four stages of the sexual response cycle as shared on pages 67–68: excitement, plateau, orgasm, and resolution. Emphasize the fact that these stages are the same whether reached by masturbation, fondling, oral sex, or sexual intercourse. Have volunteers read aloud the statements from teens about arousal that appear on page 75.

2. Have a volunteer read **Genesis 38:8–10**, which tells the story of what is sometimes called the sin of Onan. Onan was criticized, however, not for masturbation but for withdrawing his penis from Tamar before ejaculation. He was supposed to provide children for his brother's widow [Deuteronomy 25:5–6]. ASK: Why might the Hebrew Bible or Old Testament have expected a man to provide children for his brother's widow? [People did not live a long time, and children were of enormous value as a result.] Why do some people take this statement as a prohibition of masturbation?

3. Make a list of comments teens have heard others make about masturbation; put them on chalkboard or newsprint. ASK: Why are people so uncomfortable talking about masturbation? What examples of masturbation have you seen on television or in movies? Why is masturbation presented more infrequently than sexual intercourse or oral sex in the media? Why do movies and television shows that refer to masturbation often do so in a joking way? Summarize the main points from pages 68–72 on masturbation. Then ask: What benefits come to people from masturbation? Are there any dangers from masturbation? If so, what are they?

4. Direct attention to the statistics on petting or fondling and on being nude with a member of the opposite sex on page 72. ASK: Are these statistics high or low for teens in the school(s) you attend? Why don't more people talk about these activities rather than just oral sex and intercourse? The study seems to take it for granted that people will be kissing when they go out together . . . at least after the first or second time. When do you think it is all right to start kissing? What kind of sexual arousal comes when people begin longer kissing, including the insertion of their tongues into each other's mouths?

5. Share this statement which the author of the book makes at the end of page 76: *Many teens in the* Faith Matters *study told me that they were sorry they had certain experiences*

so early; no one said that he or she was sorry for delaying a particular sexual experience. Then close with prayer.

Session Five
Chapter Seven: Oral Sex and Intercourse

By the end of this session, teens should:
- have thought about the beliefs or values of other teens concerning sexual intercourse and oral sex and also thought about their own values.
- learned some factual information about sexual intercourse and oral sex.
- have thought through more carefully what is involved in having sexual intercourse or oral sex.
- have thought about what it means to think of the body as God's temple.

1. Give each teen a blank notecard and have them number from one through seven. Ask them not to put their names on the cards. Then have them write "agree" or "disagree" for each of these statements:

1. My faith community believes that premarital intercourse is wrong.

2. The Scriptures of my faith teach that premarital intercourse is wrong.

3. I personally believe that premarital intercourse is wrong.

4. My faith community believes that oral sex before marriage is wrong.

5. My faith community believes that oral sex is wrong even for people who are married.

6. The Scriptures of my faith teach that oral sex before marriage is wrong.

7. I personally believe that oral sex before marriage is wrong.

Collect the notecards for use later in the session.

2. Have the group take the "True or False?" quiz on sexual intercourse on page 78. Then look at the responses on pages 79–80. ASK: Why do you think the author inserted the "Coronary Care Alert" on page 80? What does his willingness to share this information say about his attitude toward young people? Why are some adults afraid to share this kind of information with teens?

3. Direct attention to the list of characteristics of teens who were less likely to have had intercourse that appears on page 81. Then look at the statistics about intercourse on page 82 and the quotes on pages 83–84; you might have volunteers read the quotes aloud. ASK: How do you feel about these comments? Are you surprised by how many had not had intercourse? Why or why not? Why is it easy to get the impression that "everyone" has had intercourse?

4. Have the group take the "True or False?" quiz on oral sex on pages 84–85. Then look at the responses on pages 85–86. Look at the statistics on oral sex and intercourse on page 87 and at the quotes from teens on pages 87–89; consider having volunteers read the quotes aloud. ASK: What factors create a view by some teens that oral sex is more casual and a smaller decision than intercourse? What are the dangers of that attitude? Do you think rates of oral sex and of intercourse in your school are higher, lower, or about the same as shared in this book? Why?

5. Shuffle the notecards and give them back to the teens, so that teens are not holding their own responses. Then take hand counts to see how many agreed with each statement. Compare the responses of the group to those given on page 89 of *The Gift of Sexuality*. Have volunteers read aloud the statements of teens on pages 91–92. ASK: Why do you think so many teens are *not* convinced that premarital intercourse and oral sex before marriage are wrong—even though they think that their faith communities teach that these activities are wrong before marriage? What are the dangers of having oral sex or sexual intercourse before marriage? Read **1 Corinthians 6:12–20** on the body as the temple of God. Note that this seems to especially criticize those who have sex with a prostitute. What does it suggest about the nature of sexual relationships?

6. Go over the seven points about the decision to have intercourse or oral sex that appear on pages 92–94. Summarize the statements for the group. Point out the questions to consider on pages 95–96, and provide a time of silence in which group members can reflect on their own thoughts about these questions. Then close with prayer.

Session Six
Chapter Eight: Homosexuality & Bisexuality

By the end of this session, teens should:
- have gained an understanding that homosexuality and bisexuality are sexual orientations held by many teens and adults.
- have gained empathy with the problems faced by teens who are homosexual or bisexual in terms of the secrecy with which many of them live and the harassment which many of them experience.
- have examined and thought about biblical passages which speak not only about homosexuality but also those which speak about how we relate to all persons regardless of sexual orientation.
- have thought through "A Religious Look at Homosexuality and determined with what parts of that perspective they agree.

1. Have teens use notecards to respond to the twelve "Yes or No?" statements on pages 100–101. Collect the cards, shuffle them, redistribute them, and then take hand counts to see how many indicated "yes" for each item.

> *If you find that there's considerable diversity of opinion on some of these items, do not be surprised. Point out to the group that people in congregations all over North America are struggling to determine how they feel about some of these issues. Emphasize that it is important to respect differences of opinion as you deal with this topic.*

ASK: Why do you think homosexuality is a topic of so much debate in North America? Were you surprised by any of the responses from our group to these items? Why, or why not?

2. Look at the statistics on sexual orientation from the *Faith Matters* study on page 101. As you look at those statistics, read aloud the second full paragraph on page 101 that talks about the adolescent years as a time when people form their sexual identity or orientation. Also read aloud the words in red on page 103 that talk about the suicide rate for non-heterosexual teens. Then look at the quotes from teens on pages 103–105; ask volunteers to read the quotes.

ASK: Were you surprised at the number of religious teens with a non-heterosexual orientation? Why, or why not? Why do you think homosexual or bisexual teens are more likely than heterosexual teens to have attempted suicide? Eighty-eight percent of the teens who self-identified as homosexual or bisexual indicated that their pastor or rabbi was not aware of their orientation. Forty-six percent said their parents were not aware of their orientation or struggle at identifying their orientation. What would it be like to be keeping your orientation a secret?

3. Have volunteers read aloud each of the biblical passages on pages 106–107. Share the background from *The Gift of Sexuality* on each passage. Then summarize the other perspectives on the biblical view on pages 107–109. ASK: What new information did you gain from this look at the biblical view of homosexuality? What are the implications of the Great Commandment [Luke 10:27] for how congregations should view and treat people of non-heterosexual orientation? How aware do you think adults in your congregation are of the information shared in this chapter? Would knowing some of this information cause some people to feel more positively about those of a homosexual orientation? Why, or why not?

4. Have volunteers read aloud the quotes on pages 109–111. ASK: Why do you think congregations are important to gay and lesbian teens even when they do not always feel acceptance there? Why is it important to help homosexual and bisexual teens feel welcome in the congregation? How can they be helped to feel more welcome than they currently are?

Pages 112–115 contain many quotes about connections teens have with persons of a non-heterosexual orientation. You may not have time to have all of these quotes read aloud, but have at least a few of them shared. ASK: What would it be like to have a mother or father who was homosexual? [There is a good possibility someone in your group may be in that situation. Don't put that person under any pressure to respond, but be sure to affirm anything that he or she says.] How are gay persons treated in the school you attend?

5. Focus attention on pages 115–116 on people who are transgender. Summarize that material for the group. ASK: What do you think it would be like to be a person who is transgender? Why is it difficult for many people to understand persons who are transgender? [Keep in mind during the discussion that there could be a person in your group who is transgender.]

6. Then look at the five statements that constitute "A Religious Look at Homosexuality" on pages 117–120. Offer your own summary, or have volunteers provide a summary of these statements. ASK: Do you think that many adults in your congregation are aware of the kind of perspective on homosexuality that is a part of these statements? Is there anything in these statements that represents a new or different perspective for you about homosexuality? If so, what? Why is it important for us as religious persons to attempt to better understand homosexuality and to be accepting of homosexual persons? Close with prayer.

Session Seven
Chapter Nine: The Bible &
Religious Beliefs

By the end of this session, teens should:
- have an understanding of four guidelines that can help them in their own biblical exploration.
- have been exposed to a broad range of biblical teachings that relate directly to sexuality or that relate to the way in which we treat one another in all relationships.
- have thought about the role that the faith community can play in helping people understand sexuality.

1. Begin by having the group do a crossword puzzle on the Bible and Sexuality. Make photocopies of the questions and the puzzle that appear on the next two pages, and have people work on the puzzle in pairs or triads. Here are the answers:

Across
   1. Solomon
   2. thigh or loins
   4. lovers
   6. passion
 10. bestiality
 12. bishops or pastors
 13. adultery
 15. flesh

Down
   3. known
   5. Jacob
   7. concubine
   8. remarry
   9. women
 11. incest
 13. angels
 14. condemn

Across

1. _____ had 700 wives and 300 concubines.
2. In passages like Genesis 24:2, the _____ is used as a euphemism (or word substitute) for saying penis and testicles.
4. The Song of Solomon talks about the experiences of two _____ who are apparently not married.
6. Although Paul speaks positively of celibacy, it is clear in 1 Corinthians 7:8–9 that he feels it is better to marry than to burn up with _____.
10. Exodus 22:19 clearly prohibits _____.
12. 1 Timothy 3:2, 12 and Titus 1:6 clearly assume that _____, deacons, and elders are married.
13. Hebrews 13:4 speaks against _____.
15. Ephesians 5:31 says that a man and a woman, joined in marriage, become one _____.

Down

3. In passages like Genesis 19:8, instead of saying that someone has (or has not) had sexual intercourse, the speaker (writer) says that the person has (or has not) _____ a member of the opposite sex.
5. According to Genesis 29:21–30:13, this person had two wives and two concubines.
7. A _____ had official status in Old Testament times, and men did sleep with such persons but their offspring did not have the same status as a wife's children.
8. According to 1 Timothy 5:14, a widow should _____.
9. Proverbs 31:3 advises not giving a man's strength to _____.
11. Passages like Leviticus 18:6–18 clearly prohibit _____.
13. According to Mark 12:25, those who rise from the dead do not marry because they are like _____.
14. In John 8:2–11, Jesus will not _____ a woman who had committed adultery.

After you've shared the answers, ASK: What information surprised you in this exercise? What did you learn about the Bible and sexuality through completing this puzzle?

2. Summarize the four guidelines that appear on pages 124–125, or have volunteers in the group summarize them. ASK: Why is it important for us to look at biblical passages through our own powers of reason and in light of our own experience? Why doesn't the Bible speak more directly to some things like artificial insemination and stem cell research? How do you feel about the concept that some omissions in Scripture might be intentional?

3. Divide into small groups [perhaps three or four persons in a group] to look at the passages and information on pages 125–128. You might want to put these questions on chalkboard or newsprint to guide the small groups:
  * Which of these passages do you find most interesting? Why?
  * Which passages do you find most disturbing? Why?
  * Which passages do you find most helpful? Why?

Then have the same small groups go through the nine guidelines on pages 129–131, answering these questions:
  * What are the three guidelines that your group considers the most important? Why?
  * Are there any guidelines that make you uncomfortable or with which you disagree? If so, why?
  * Are there any additional guidelines that you would add to the list? If so, why?

4. Then provide time for each small group to report to the larger group on some of their conclusions.

5. Summarize some of the main points in pages 132–136 on how congregations do and do not help teens in these areas. ASK: Why do you think clergy, youth advisors or teachers, and teens gave such different ratings to the job the congregation does on preparing youth in each of the three areas (sexual information, marriage, and parenting)? How do you think our own congregation does in helping prepare young people in those three areas? What are some of the barriers to more frank discussion of these concerns in congregations? How can teens help adults in congregations be more responsible? Close with prayer.

Session Eight
Chapter Ten: Unwanted Sex

By the end of this session, teens should:
- have become more aware that unwanted sexual experiences happen to many teens and can happen to them.
- have a better understanding of the role that peer pressure, alcohol, drugs, and other factors can play in making a person more vulnerable to unwanted sexual experiences.
- be aware of steps they can take to make it far less likely that they will be a victim of an unwanted sexual experience.
- be aware of what they should do if they are a victim of such an experience.

Be alert for a television show or movie that deals with rape or other unwanted sexual experiences. Consider the possibility of using a film clip on DVD or videotape as the introduction to the whole session or to a particular activity in the session.

Be sensitive to the reality that you may well have teens in your group who have had unwanted sexual experiences.

1. Use notecards to have people respond to the eight "Yes or No?" items on pages 138 concerning unwanted sexual experiences. Collect the notecards, shuffle them, and then redistribute them. Take hand counts and mark on chalkboard or newsprint the number who answered "yes" to each item. For the purposes of the hand counts, have people respond from the card they are holding rather than their personal response.

ASK: Did the number answering "yes" to any of the questions surprise you? Why, or why not? Why is it difficult to talk about rape and other unwanted sexual experiences?

2. Read aloud or have a volunteer read aloud **Genesis 19:1–11** about the unwanted experience of Lot's daughters. Why did Lot offer his daughters to the men? What does his willingness to offer his daughters say about his respect for the daughters? In what ways is it possible for parents today to contribute to unwanted sexual experiences for their children? [Failure to provide enough information about protection; failure to listen and be supportive; failure to adequately supervise; etc.] How can parents help make it less likely that a son or daughter will have an unwanted sexual experience?

3. Direct attention to the statistics about unwanted sexual experiences on page 139, noting in particular that by the 11th and 12th grades, 31% of females have had an unwanted experience. Have volunteers read the quotes that appear on pages 139–142. ASK: How can social pressure and peer expectations push a person into sexual experiences for which he or she is not ready? How do male and female stereotypes contribute to unwanted sexual experiences? To what extend do you think teens in your community feel under pressure to participate in sexual activity?

4. Focus attention on the types of unwanted sexual activity listed at the top of page 143. Note that there are persons who have had unwanted sexual intercourse but did not want to call it rape; the bullets on page 143 share some of the reasons. ASK: Why do you think a person might not want to call unwanted sexual intercourse rape?

Go through the list of bulleted points on pages 145–146 on factors among teens who had unwanted sexual experiences. ASK: Which of those seem especially problematic for people you know? Page 146 shares that 26.3% of the teens in the *Faith Matters* study were using alcohol or drugs on at least one occasion when they had an unwanted sexual experience. Why do you think alcohol or drugs make it more likely that a person may have an unwanted sexual experience? Many people feel that no teen should ever use alcohol or drugs. Do you agree or disagree with that position? How do you feel about adults using alcohol or drugs?

Have a volunteer read aloud the experience of the 10th grade female with a college sophomore as described in pages 147–148. ASK: What are the problems with dating someone who is much older than you are or who is no longer in high school?

5. Go carefully through the seven points about prevention and what to do if something bad happens as given on pages 151–155. ASK: Which of the prevention strategies are most difficult to implement? Why? Do most of your friends know about the prevention strategies shared in this book? Why, or why not?

Emphasize to teens that you are available to talk with them privately if they have been a victim of an unwanted sexual experience of any kind. Be clear that you will help them even if this is an experience that has happened with a member of their family or with someone in the congregation. Close with prayer.

If you find that you need help in working with a teen who has been through a tragic experience, remember that resources include clergy, sexuality educators, psychologists, rape crisis centers, and organizations like those listed in the "Resources" section of this book. There are professional counselors who specialize in helping people who have had such experiences.

Session Nine
Chapter Eleven: Contraception, Pregnancy, STDs, and Abortion

By the end of this session, teens should:
- have gained an understanding of some of the means of contraception that are available.
- have gained an understanding of sexually transmitted diseases and how they can be avoided.
- have come to understand that the decision to have an abortion does not have to be faced if one avoids unplanned pregnancy.
- have considered the reasons why a religious person needs to be responsible in any kind of sexual activity.

Unwanted pregnancies, HIV, and abortions are all topics that get covered in television shows and movies. If there is a show or movie that is currently popular, you may be able to use a film clip from it. Or you might even decide to schedule an extra session to show and discus the entire show or movie.

Another approach to this session could be to have a professional sexuality educator, a nurse, or a medical doctor come to talk about these topics. He or she may be able to bring samples of the contraceptive and protective devices discussed.

1. Have teens take the "True or False?" quiz on page 158, putting their responses on notecards without their names. If teens have already read the chapter, they should do very well on the quiz! Collect the notecards, and shuffle them. You'll redistribute them later in the session.

2. Direct attention to the statistics on pregnancy on page 159. Note that the pregnancy rate is much higher among sexually active teens than it is for the total *Faith Matters* sample. ASK: Are you surprised by the percentage of religious teens who became pregnant? Why, or why not? What could their parents and congregations have done to help them avoid pregnancy?

Then talk about the fact that 50% of the teens in the study who became pregnant ended the pregnancy with an abortion. ASK: What are some of the factors that you think caused them to decide on abortion rather than keeping the baby or having the baby adopted? Look at the five cases on pages 162 and 163. In which of those situations do you think abortion would be most justified? In which of the situations do you think abortion is least justified? How do you feel about this statement from page 163: "We seek to create a world in which abortion is safe, legal, accessible, and rare"?

3. Point out the signs of pregnancy on page 165. Then look at the options as described on pages 166–167. ASK: Which of those options seem to you most consistent with religious faith? Which of those options will have the least negative impact on the lives of the parents of the child?

Redistribute the notecards from the opening activity. Look at the responses to the "True or False?" quiz on pages 170–171, and compare them with the responses on the notecards people are holding.

Pages 172–177 describe twelve different approaches to contraception. Have group members turn their notecards over, and ask each person to write down on the left-hand side of the card the three means of contraception that seem the best and on the right-hand side the three means of contraception that seem to them the least good. Let them interpret "best" and "least good" in the way that they want. It may be a balance of effectiveness, convenience, and ease of obtaining; or they may decide to put all the weight on a single variable like the percentage of effectiveness. Collect the cards, shuffle them, and redistribute them. Use hand-counts to find out which methods were most often listed as "best" and which were most often listed as "least good." ASK: Why did the instructions use the term "least good" rather than ineffective or bad? How many teens have as much information about approaches to contraception as was presented in *The Gift of Sexuality*? Why it

111

is important for teens to have this information? How do you feel about this statement: "Abstinence is the only 100% effective means of contraception"?

4. Have teens take the "True or False?" quiz on pages 178–179 about sexually transmitted diseases. Then have them divide into small groups to talk about the answers that are on pages 179–183. You might put these questions on chalkboard or newsprint for discussion in the small groups:

- About which sexually transmitted disease did you know the most before reading this chapter? About which did you know the least?

- What sexually transmitted diseases do you think are . most common in your community among teens?

- What responsibilities do people have for preventing sexually transmitted diseases if they choose to be sexually active?

5. Read **Deuteronomy 28:4** on children as a sign of God's blessings. ASK: Are children who result from unplanned pregnancies any less a sign of God's blessings? Why, or why not? What does the reality that children are a blessing of God suggest about the importance of being responsible in sexual relationships?

Read the final lines on page 184, and then close with prayer.

Session Ten
Chapter Twelve: A Guide to Dating

By the end of this session, teens should:
*   better understand the difference between those factors that attract us to another person and those factors that make for a long-lasting relationship.
*   be better able to identify both the joys and the concerns that are part of a dating relationship.
*   be more aware of the factors to consider in choosing to become more serious in a dating relationship.
*   have thought about how a religious person should treat his or her partner in a dating relationship.

*Be sure to note the opening words of Chapter 12 in **The Gift of Sexuality** about issues of terminology concerning "dating." Dating may not be the word some of the teens in your group use to describe their romantic relationships. Be sensitive to that possibility as you lead discussion on this chapter.*

Think in advance about how to handle the role plays that are suggested in the last activity of the session. Who would be the best persons for these parts? If you think the role playing will be too awkward for your group, then just discuss the situations that are described.

1. Have teens complete the "Thoughts about Dating" exercise on pages 186–187. Divide into small groups for discussion. You may wish to put these instructions on chalkboard or newsprint for the small groups:

*   Go around your small group and have people share responses to the seven items as they feel comfortable

doing. Share reasons for your responses as you want. It's fine to say, "I pass" in response to any item.

• How much do you need to know about a person before going out? Do you think it is important to feel like you could be really serious about a person before going out with that person? Why, or why not?

• What are the dangers of meeting someone through the Internet? Why should you protect personal information when in Internet chat rooms? Under what circumstances, if any, should you ever come face-to-face with someone you met on the Internet?

Give the small groups opportunity to share any thoughts they wish with the larger group.

2. Pages 188–191 give ten recommendations on getting someone to go out with you. ASK: With which of these recommendations do you most strongly agree? Why? Are there any with which you disagree? Why? What recommendations would you add to the list?

Make a list of the things that teens in the group think are most enjoyable to do on a date; list the ideas on chalkboard or newsprint. Compare that to the list on pages 191–192.

3. Break into three groups. Assign each group a different focus:

• "Equal Dating" [pages 192–193].

• "Getting Serious" [pages 193–195].

• "Breaking Up" [pages 196–198].

Ask each group to summarize the most important concepts from the assigned section and any additional thoughts they have and then report back to the total group.

4. Look at the "lines" used on pages 195–196. ASK: What other lines have you heard? What is wrong with using lines like these to try to get the other person to do what you want? When have you known adults to be guilty of using lines?

5. Read **Luke 10:27**. [This same verse has been considered in other sessions because it has so many implications for how we treat others.] Then have volunteers do role plays and talk about the implications of that verse for each situation. Role plays:

- A few girlfriends have heard that someone they know went "all the way" on Saturday night. They are discussing her actions when she joins the group. What happens?

Discuss: What was the reaction of the group when the girl walked up? Would this same situation ever take place among a group of guys? What double standards of behavior exist for males and females? What are the implications of Luke 10:27 for this situation?

- A few fellows are standing in the locker room discussing the dates they had on Friday night. Tom did nothing but kiss Karen good-night; but when the guys ask him if he "saw any action," he is too embarrassed to tell the truth. What does he say?

Discuss: What was the reaction of the guys to Tom's account? In what ways may they see Karen differently now? What has Tom gained by not telling the truth? How might this hurt him or hurt Karen in the future? What are the implications of Luke 10:27 for this situation?

- David and Jill go out together for the first time. Jill has heard that David is "really hot." She starts telling David what she is interested in doing sexually and finds out that he is uncomfortable with what she is suggesting and with her taking the initiative to talk about these things.

Discuss: Did it seem strange to you that Jill was the one making the verbal advances? Why does the first time out seem too early to discuss sexual expectations? What are the problems with waiting too long to do so? What is the appropriate time for such conversations? What role did gossip or rumor play in what happened? What are the implications of Luke 10:27 for this situation?

Close with prayer.

Session Eleven
Chapter Thirteen: A Guide to Marriage

By the end of this session, teens should:
- have thought about the meaning of some of the biblical teachings about marriage and considered what it means to see a life partner as a "soul mate."
- have thought about some of the factors that are most important to them in a potential marriage partner and about what factors indicate a person is "ready" for marriage.
- have raised some questions about the extravagant wedding celebrations that have become the norm for many people in North America.

If you are going to prepare a videotape or a DVD for the first activity, you'll need to do that in advance. The alternative opening activity involving magazines with articles about weddings also requires gathering some materials.

If you are going to have group members do the parent interviews for the session after this one, have copies prepared that you can distribute at this session.

1. <u>Option one</u>: Show a videotape or DVD that you have prepared (or had a class member prepare) which shows a few short scenes about marriage from television or current movies. For example, you might include:

- An engagement ring advertisement.

- A scene from a movie that shows the complexity and/or the beauty of a large wedding.

- A credit card advertisement focused on a newly married couple or a family paying for a wedding.

- A sitcom or daytime soap scene about a wedding or about wedding planning.

ASK: To what extent do advertisements, movies, magazines, and other media create the impression that a wedding should be large; that engagement rings should be expensive; and that weddings should be "perfect"? If you have been close to someone who was planning a wedding, what challenges did that person seem to experience in the planning process? How do you feel about the statement: "Couples should spend more time planning the marriage than planning the wedding"?

Option two: Have an assortment of magazines available that are likely to have information and advertisements in them about weddings. Obviously magazines that are focused just on that topic are one source, but weddings get mentioned in a large number of publications (*People* and *Entertainment Weekly*, for example, often include information on celebrity weddings). Let people work in groups of two to four persons to find advertisements and articles about weddings that they find interesting. Then invite them to share with the rest of the group. Use the same questions for discussion that appear under Option one.

Option three: Go straight to the discussion questions that appear under Option one.

2. Read aloud **Genesis 2:24**: "Therefore a man leaves his father and mother and cleaves to his wife, and they become one flesh." Then direct attention back to pages 125–128. Have group members call out passages that relate in any way to marriage, and make a list of those on chalkboard or newsprint.

ASK: What do you think the Bible teaches us about marriage? It appears that the concept of marriage changed some during the history of the Bible since we find references to Solmon, for example, having so many wives and concubines but find no references to multiple wives in the New Testament. Why do you think the concept of marriage changed during the years covered by the Bible? What do you think are the most important things that the Bible says about marriage?

3. Summarize for the group the concept of "soul mate" as found on pages 201–204. Note the final paragraph:

"If you get married, the person whom you choose for a spouse, if you make a true commitment to that person, will become your soul mate. It isn't a matter of finding the *one* right person. It is a matter of making a commitment to the person you choose. When you make that commitment, God helps that person become your soul mate."

ASK: What are the dangers of thinking that God has intended only one specific person as the one you are to marry? To what extent do you think our society reinforces that concept? How do you feel about the author's concept that one's commitment is really what determines who becomes your soul mate?

4. Have group members complete the exercise on marriage and life goals that appears on pages 204–205. Then invite people to share responses to the items in groups of two to four persons.

Then have the small groups look at the nine guidelines on being ready for marriage that appear on pages 206–209. Put these questions for small groups discussion on chalkboard or newsprint:

• Which of these guidelines do group members think are most important? Why?

• Are there any with which you disagree? If so, why?

• Are there any that should be added? If so, why?

5. Summarize for the group pages 209–211 on the physical and spiritual dimensions of marriage. ASK: According to the author, how do the Jewish and the Christian faith view the body and sexual pleasure? What does it mean to be a partner with God in creation?

Then focus attention on the four points about weddings on pages 211–216. ASK: The author says "We understandably are influenced by weddings that we have attended or in which we have participated. That's normal. Be careful, however, that you don't get caught in the trap of feeling that you must do your wedding the same way as other people have done their weddings." How much influence do you think the weddings of others have on people who are about to plan their own wedding?

What are the dangers of that influence? What do you think about the author's suggestions for making weddings a little simpler and less expensive? What other "outside of the box" ideas for weddings can you identify?

Close with prayer.

Session Twelve
Chapter Fourteen: A Guide to Parenting

By the end of this session, teens should:
*   have a better understanding of the reasons why parenting is such an important task and major responsibility.
*   have considered some of the characteristics of good parents.
*   be motivated to learn more about what it means to be a good parent.
*   better understand that being a good parent is a matter of religious importance.

The following page has "Ask Your Parents" questions which you can distribute to group members in advance of the meeting so that they can interview their parents.

1. If you distributed the "Ask Your Parents" questions to group members last week, provide time for them to share some of the things that they learned, either as a large group or in small groups of three or four persons.

If you did not distribute the questions in advance, then try having people share how they *think* their parents would answer the questions!

2. Focus attention on the "Waiting to Have a Child" section on pages 218–221. Make a list of the reasons for waiting on chalkboard or newsprint. Then make a list of reasons why some people go ahead and have children while still very young themselves. ASK: Which of the reasons for waiting seem most important to you? Why? What could be done to help people better understand what is involved in having a child?

Ask Your Parents. . . .

1. If you are comfortable telling me, how did I come into existence? Had you made a conscious decision that you were ready to have a child, or did I come along unexpectedly?

2. What was I like as a baby? Was I basically fussy, or basically sweet, or a mixture of both? What did you like best about me? Was there anything I did that made you crazy? If so, what?

3. How stressful is it to be a parent? What things have I done that were stressful for you? Did I cause more stress for you when I was a baby, or when I was a young child, or when I became a teenager?

4. As you look back, what are the best choices that you think you've made as a parent? Why? Are there choices you made that you wish you could change? If so, what are they and why?

5. What do you wish you had known about before you became a parent? What things would have made it easier to be a parent?

6. What advice would you give me for the time when I become a parent myself?

3. Focus attention on the "Twelve Characteristics of Good Parents" on pages 221–228. Assign some or all of the characteristics to teams of two or three persons. Ask each team to come up with a short skit or role play that shows a "bad" parent violating the characteristic. For characteristic number two, for example, on "set a good example," have a parent acting as though smoking while telling a son or daughter to avoid drugs.

4. Have the skits or role plays presented to the whole group. When the skits have been presented, ASK: Which of the good characteristics seem to you the most difficult ones to live out in daily life? Why? Which of the characteristics do you think you would be best at? Why? Which of the characteristics do you think you would be worst at? Why?

5. Have a volunteer read aloud **Matthew 19:18–15**. ASK: Why do you suppose the disciples initially scolded people for bringing children to Jesus? What do the words and actions of Jesus say about the importance that he places on children? What does this suggest about the responsibility that we have when we are parents? Close with prayer.

Session Thirteen
What Next?

By the end of this session, teens should:
* have reflected on what they have learned during this study.
* have identified some of the specific things they want to do in response to what they have learned.
* have talked about how they may be able to influence people in the congregation to do more to help others be prepared for dating, sexual decision-making, marriage, and parenting.

This session challenges teens to think about what they have learned and also to think about needs in the congregation. You should read through the questions in advance to see if there is further information you should get about policies and programs that already exist in your church.

1. Provide a few minutes for teens to complete the "What Do You Know?" activity on pages 10–12 of *The Gift of Sexuality.* They completed this same activity near the start of Session One. They should mark an X on each line indicating how characteristic that activity is of them with **7** indicating "very characteristic" and **1** indicating "not at all characteristic.

Don't put individuals on the spot to share their responses to those items. ASK: How do you think your responses compare to the ones you made at the start of this study? In which areas do you feel you have learned the most or gained the most during this study? Why? Are there areas in which you still would like to learn a great deal more? If so, what are they?

2. Invite teens to call out the main things they have learned or the things that they plan to do differently as a result of this study. Write those on chalkboard or newsprint.

Then ask them to identify the topics that they would most like to know more about or talk more about. List those on chalkboard or newsprint as well, and talk about how opportunities to do that might come about.

3. Go back to pages 132–136 in *The Gift of Sexuality*. Those pages talk about the role of the congregation in helping teens in these areas. ASK:

- What should our congregation be doing to help younger children have the information they need about their bodies and about being safe?

- What should our congregation be doing in terms of outreach to teens in the community who need help?

- Does our congregation do anything to help people who are already married strengthen their relationships? If so, what? If not, what might be done?

- Every community has GLBT persons, and almost all congregations do. What could our congregation do to be more affirming of GLBT persons? What could our congregation to do be more helpful to GLBT persons? How could we as a group help people in the congregation respond in more positive ways to GLBT people?

- Would it be helpful to have a group or class for teens that focused on marriage and parenting? Why, or why not? If it would be helpful, when should we consider having such a class or group?

- Unwanted sex can be a significant problem, even in the life of the church. Does your church have a program designed to keep people safe? If not, how might such a program be started? [Debra Haffner's book *A Time to Heal* is an excellent resource for this purpose.]

- Should our congregation have a class for parents that would help them be better prepared to help their children know the things that are needed about their bodies and sexuality? Why, or why not?

4. Based on the responses of the group to the third activity, decide together if there are any changes they would like to get

accomplished in the congregation. If so, then determine a strategy to proceed. That might include:

- Having a meeting with parents to gain their support.

- Talking to the priest, minister, rabbi, or other clergy-person to gain that person's support.

- Bringing the request to the appropriate decision-making group in the congregation.

5. Close with prayer, thanking God for the gift of sexuality and for the gift of people with whom to explore the meaning of that gift.

Resources

This "Resources" section includes most of the information shared in the "Where to Go for Help" section of *The Gift of Sexuality* but also includes some additional information that may be helpful to parents, clergy, youth workers, and other concerned adults.

The Internet

There are some sites on the Internet that provide information that may be helpful to you and to the teens about whom you care. Please keep in mind that Internet addresses change and that the management of Internet sites can also change. This information is accurate as the book goes to press:

Sex, Etc.: www.sxetc.org
This excellent site provides advice for teens about sexuality in a FAQ [Frequently Asked Question] and story format. Major topics include contraception, STDs, and sexual decision-making with additional web links for each subject. The site also covers topics like health, love and relationships, teen parenting, abortion and adoption, abuse and violence, drugs, and body image. This is a project of the "Network for Family Life Education" by Rutgers University, so you can have confidence in the accuracy of the information provided.

Teenwire: www.teenwire.com
This is also an excellent site and is managed by Planned Parenthood. It's hip with cool graphics and teen language. Topics include contraception, adoption, abortion, relationships, pregnancy, emotional and sexual issues, world views, STDs, gay issues, and more. There are also a lot of stories and topics aimed at African-American and Hispanic audiences. You can count on Planned Parenthood to offer current and accurate information on sexuality.

Coalition for Positive Sexuality: www.positive.org
This is a down-to-earth site that provides a lot of information using teen language and illustrations. It's one of the most extensive and popular on the Internet.

Cool Nurse: www.coolnurse.com
This helpful site has information on various health-related concerns including topics like STDs, pregnancy, sexual FAQs [Frequently Asked Questions], contraception, and gynecology.

Teensexuality Information Center: www.teensexuality.com
This site offers general information on sexuality issues with an extensive page of links to other sites. Topics covered include understanding your sexuality, contraception, STDs, sexual health, and sexual assault. It is aimed at an older teen crowd or college students, and the link page is very good.

I wanna know: www.iwannaknow.org
This site is managed by the American Social Health Association. It offers sexual health and STD prevention information for teens including chat, education, games, and other resources. This site is very informative and has a section for parents too.

Puberty 101: www.puberty101.com
This is a great site for puberty issues including topics such as circumcision, penis size, wet dreams, sexual feelings, love, and underarm hair. The site also covers STDs, mental health, and drugs.

Campaign For Our Children Inc.: www.cfoc.org/teenguide
This site has a pro-life and an abstinence slant. The site includes an educator resource center and media/press area. Topics include abstinence, contraceptives, sexuality, date rape, STDs, and sexual abuse.

Scarleteen: www.scarleteen.com
This site is aimed at teenage girls and has a magazine feel to the layout and presentation. It promotes itself as delivering contemporary teen sex education and is a pro-choice site. Topics include sexuality, infection, reproduction, health, relationships, gay issues, and a crisis hotline. There is a section for parents.

gURL: www.gurl.com
This is another site aimed toward teen girls with a contemporary magazine feel. It covers topics such as being yourself, beliefs, body image, dating, health, emotions, gynecology, birth control, date rape, petting, and abortion. It includes lots of polls and resources.

Boys Under Attack: www.boysunderattack.com
This is a fairly conservative Christian site. Topics include puberty, erections, gay issues, lust, pornography, and virginity. The site also covers God's love and has an adult section.

Sistahs: www.mysistahs.org
This is a very interesting site especially aimed at adolescents of color and heavy on disease prevention. Health topics are covered as well as poetry and essays.

PFLAG: www.critpath.org/pflag-talk
This is a large site dedicated to various gay issues concerning education, support, and advocacy. The site offers links, resources, a talk/chat line, and more. This is managed by the PFLAG [Parents, Family, and Friends of Lesbians and Gays] organization.

Girl.Mom: www.girlmom.com
This is a site for the support of teenage mothers and is supported by the Coalition for the Empowerment of Teen Parents. The site is written by teens for teens and includes lots of stores, articles, and essays.

Telephone Numbers

Some of the websites listed above also offer toll-free numbers. In this section I want to briefly highlight some additional telephone numbers that could be valuable to you and to the teens about whom you care.

Backline: 1-888-493-0092. Backline offers a toll free, confidential talk line for women and their loved ones to explore pregnancy, abortion, adoption, and parenting. Callers from all over the United States can speak to an Advocate about the wide range of feelings and questions they may have and receive support, resources, and tools for communication and decision-making. The telephone number is the most important resource, but they also have a website at www.yourbackline.org

Other numbers:

National Eating Disorders Association: 1-800-931-2237

National Drug and Alcohol Treatment Hotline 1-800-662-HELP

National Domestic Violence Hotline 1-800-799-7233

National Child Abuse Hotline 1-800-4-A-CHILD

National Youth Crisis Hotline 1-800-HIT-HOME

National Adolescent Suicide Hotline 1-800-621-4000

The Teen AIDS Hotline 1-800-440-TEEN

National AIDS Hot Line at 1-800-342-AIDS

Organizations and Resources

Planned Parenthood. There are Planned Parenthood affiliates all over the United States. Many people associate Planned Parenthood so strongly with the abortion debate that they fail to recognize Planned Parenthood's extensive involvement in sexuality education with the provision of accurate information to people of all ages. You can look up the local office in your phone book or call 800-230-7526. Planned Parenthood Federation of America, 434 West 33rd St. New York, NY 10001. www.plannedparenthood.org

Christian Community. That's the organization responsible for the book that you hold in your hands. Christian Community focuses on research and resource development to benefit congregations and the communities in which they minister. In addition to research and development on teens and sexuality, the organization has also developed resources on faith-sharing, hospitality, worship, and stewardship. 6404 S. Calhoun Street, Fort Wayne, Indiana 46807. 800-774-3360. DadofTia@aol.com; www.churchstuff.com

The other organizations listed here are somewhat more for adults who are looking at this book and want resources:

The FaithTrust Institute. This organization works with faith-based institutions to address sexual and domestic violence. They offer books, videos, and seminars. They can refer victims to sources of counseling in a local area. 2400 N. 45th Street, Suite 10, Seattle, Washington 98103. 206-634-1903. www.faithtrustinstitute.org

The Black Church Initiative. This is a project of the Religious Coalition for Reproductive Choice and has the goal of breaking the silence about sexuality in African-American churches. They have sexuality education curricula for both adults and teens, and they hold an annual National Black Religious Summit on Sexuality. 1025 Vermont Avenue, N.W., Suite 1130, Washington, DC. www.rcrc.org

The Abortion Conversation Project. The Abortion Conversation Project is committed to eliminating the stigma of abortion by creating new ways and opportunities to talk about abortion honestly and publicly. Their website and other programs offer conversations that do not demonize those with differing views. They seek to create safe spaces for women and men to consider what is best for their lives. 1718 Connecticut Avenue, NW, Suite 700, Washington, DC 20009. 202-319-0055. www.abortion conversation.com

The Religious Institute for Sexual Morality, Justice, and Healing. This is an ecumenical, interfaith organization dedicated to advocating for sexual health, education, and justice in faith communities and society. They offer resources, consulting, and seminars to help congregations become sexually healthy faith communities. They partner with Christian Community on many projects. 304 Main Avenue, #335, Norwalk, Connecticut 06851. 203-840-1148. www.religiousinstitute.org

National Campaign to Prevent Teen Pregnancy. This organization brings together people from many different fields in cooperative efforts to prevent teen pregnancy. They offer a wide range of resources, including some developed especially for religious institutions. They have a website packed with helpful information including materials you can download without charge. 1776 Massachusetts Avenue, N.W., #200, Washington, DC 20036. 202-478-8518. www.teenpregnancy.org

SIECUS: Sexuality Information and Education Council of the United States. This organization offers a large number of resources in the area of sexuality education and has helped set standards for sexuality education that have influenced many people and organizations, including the author of this book. Suite 350, 130 West 42nd Street, New York, New York 10036. 212-819-9770. www.siecus.org

The Health Action AIDS Campaign. This project of **Physicians for Human Rights** mobilizes U.S. medical, public health, and nursing professionals in the effort to bring additional leadership and resources from the United States to the global struggle against the AIDS pandemic. Health Action AIDS promotes policies and programs that are based in sound science and human rights principles. Health professionals from across the U.S. are encouraged to get involved. 2 Arrow Street Suite 301, Cambridge, MA 02138. 617-301-4200. www.phrusa.org or www.HealthActionAIDS.org

The Center for Sexuality and Religion. This organization focuses on the education of clergy in the area of sexuality and works in cooperation with seminaries. 987 Old Eagle School Road, Suite 719, Wayne, Pennsylvania 19087-1708. 610-995-0341. www.CTRSR.org

Advocates for Youth. Established in 1980 as the Center for Population Options, Advocates for Youth champions efforts to help young people make informed and responsible decisions about their reproductive and sexual health. Advocates believes it can best serve the field by boldly advocating for a more positive and realistic approach to adolescent sexual health. They offer extensive training programs for youth as advocates and peer educators, and they work to influence public policy around the country. 2000 M Street NW, Suite 750 Washington, DC 20036. 202-419-3420. www.advocatesforyouth.org/

Our Whole Lives. This is a comprehensive sexuality education curriculum designed for use in faith-based institutions. It was developed by the Unitarian Universalist Association and the United Church of Christ and is the most complete and accurate curriculum available for religious communities. *Our Whole Lives* is a series of sexuality education curricula for five age groups: grades K–1, grades 4–6, grades 7–9, grades 10–12, and adults. *Our Whole Lives* helps participants make informed and responsible decisions about their sexual health and behavior. It equips participants with accurate, age-appropriate information in six subject areas: human development, relationships, personal skills, sexual behavior, sexual health, and society and culture. Grounded in a holistic view of sexuality, *Our Whole Lives* provides not only facts about anatomy and human development, but helps participants to clarify their values, build interpersonal skills, and understand the spiritual, emotional, and social aspects of sexuality. This is excellent material for churches. www.uua.org/owl/what.html or www.ucc.org/justice/owl

Group Publishing. This is a nondenominational organization that provides a variety of resources for Christian congregations including some which deal with sexuality. You'll find many helpful materials here. P.O. Box 481, Loveland, Colorado 80539. 800-447-1070. www.grouppublishing.com

Youth Specialties. This is another nondenominational organization offering a variety of resources for youth work including some that deal with sexuality. 300 S. Pierce Street, El Cajon, California 92029. 619-440-2333. www.youthspecialties.com

Books from Christian Community and LifeQuest

Your own denomination likely offers resources to help youth in the area of sexuality; space doesn't permit a full listing here. The book *A Time to Speak* by Debra Haffner offers extensive information about denominational perspectives on sexuality education. The following resources are all available from Christian Community and LifeQuest, the publishers of this book:

Faith Matters by Steve Clapp, Kristen Leverton Helbert, and Angela Zizak. This book shares the results of Christian Community's national study of 5,819 teenagers representing a broad range of religious traditions, ethnic backgrounds, economic levels, and geographic locations. This book provides the full survey results, including lengthy comments from teens. This book is an especially great asset in helping congregational leaders make the decision to do more in the area of sexuality education. $16 each; $9 each for 10 or more copies.

The Gift of Sexuality: Empowerment for Religious Teens by Steve Clapp. This is the book written for youth which is the companion to the book you are holding in your hands. $16 each; $9 each for 10 or more.

Adult Guide to The Gift of Sexuality: Empowerment for Religious Teens by Steve Clapp. This *is* the book you are holding in your hands. Additional copies are available at $14 each; $9 each for 10 or more.

A Time to Heal: Protecting Children & Ministering to Sex Offenders by The Reverend Debra W. Haffner. This important book provides the tools that faith communities need to:
- determine under what circumstances, if any, a convicted sex offender may be involved in the congregation
- determine how to respond if someone in the congregation is accused of a sexual offense
- be sensitive to and supportive of persons in the congregation who have been victims of abuse

- develop and implement strategies that will keep children in the congregation safe and which will prevent sexual abuse from happening.

This resource can be used by clergy, lay leadership in churches and synagogues, denominational executives, regional judicatory executives, correctional officials, judges, parole officers, probation officers, and treatment providers. $12 each; $9 each for 10 or more copies.

A Time to Speak: Faith Communities and Sexuality Education by The Reverend Debra W. Haffner and Kate M. Ott. This book affirms the unique role of congregations in providing sexuality education. This publication explains:

- why religious institutions must be involved in sexuality education
- how churches can provide sexuality education in the congregational environment
- how churches can support sexuality education in the community.

This resource includes an extensive listing of denominational statements on sexuality education and a thorough guide to sexuality resources available from many denominations. This book is a great planning tool for the local congregation. $13 each.

A Time to Build: Creating Sexually Healthy Faith Communities by The Reverend Debra W. Haffner. This book provides:

- characteristics of sexually healthy faith communities
- characteristics of sexually healthy religious professionals
- guidance on "safe congregation" policies, including the prevention of sexual abuse and sexual harassment
- ideas for worship services and sermons on sexuality.
- guidance on sexuality counseling by trained religious leaders
- strategies for sexuality education for children, youth, and adults
- suggestions on how congregations can advocate for sexual and spiritual wholeness in their communities. $13 each.

The preceding books are all available now. Christian Community and LifeQuest have several related titles in development that you may want to know about:

What's Religion Got to Do with It? Sexuality, Violence, and Empowerment by Steve Clapp and Stacey Sellers. This book grows out of a two-year consultation and deals with the too-common silence of the religious community on issues of sexuality and violence. The book includes practical strategies for people wanting to deal in healthier ways with anger and sexuality and explores the ways in which anger and assertiveness can empower our lives.

Marriage and Parenting: A Guide for Religious Teens by Steve Clapp and Holly Sprunger. This book is especially designed for teens who have read *The Gift of Sexuality* and would like to be better prepared for their future roles as marriage partners and parents. The book helps teens understand the factors that contribute to a healthy marriage and the factors that make for good parenting in significantly greater detail than was possible in *The Gift of Sexuality*.

The Teen to Teen Network by Steve Clapp and Stacey Sellers. This is a concise book for teens that provides basic information about sexuality from a spiritual perspective. It's especially designed for broad distribution and for teens to pass to other teens.

GLBT Rights: Strategies for People of Faith by multiple authors. This manual is growing out of a major research project that looks at ways religious people can make a difference for GLBT persons. The manual explores ways to help congregations better understand sexual orientation and GLBT rights. This is a practical manual that will help clergy and other religious leaders who want to create greater understanding and compassion for GLBT persons as well as those working to protect the rights of all persons in our society.

Women, Sexuality, and Religion: Healthy Reproductive Choices for Women of Faith by Steve Clapp and Angela Zizak. This book is especially aimed at women in their late teens and early twenties. It looks at reproductive rights and reproductive choices from a spiritual perspective.

LifeQuest and Christian Community
6404 S. Calhoun Street
Fort Wayne, Indiana 46807
800-774-3360
DadofTia@aol.com